PHYSICAL EDUCATION FOR CHILDREN
WITH PERCEPTUAL-MOTOR
LEARNING DISABILITIES

ROBERT W. HARVAT

Denver Public Schools

PHYSICAL EDUCATION FOR CHILDREN
WITH PERCEPTUAL-MOTOR
LEARNING DISABILITIES

CHARLES E. MERRILL PUBLISHING COMPANY
Columbus, Ohio   *A Bell & Howell Company*

THE SLOW LEARNER SERIES
edited by Newell C. Kephart, Ph.D.

International Standard Book Number: 0–675–09901–3

Library of Congress Catalog Card Number: 78–158072

LB
1067
·H3

1 2 3 4 5 6 7 8 9 10—75 74 73 72 71
Printed in the United States of America

Foreword

In recent years there has been increasing interest in motor learning in relation to the overall learning of the child. Learning is the result of an interaction between the child and his environment. Such an interaction demands response on the part of the child—a movement, initially overt and finally, as a body of response information develops, non-overt. Such movement must not only occur, but it must occur voluntarily and in relation to the particular impingement of the environment which is presenting the learning situation. Learning can only occur when a stimulus and a response become related. To over-look either end of this interaction is to impede learning.

Not only are specific voluntary movement responses to isolated stimuli important to learning, but controlled movements over time are equally important. Child development specialists have for many years emphasized the importance of exploration and manipulation in the learning of the young child. Through such continuous exploration of spaces and objects, the bases for such essential concepts as form perception and space structure are laid. Such concepts, however, are dependent upon continuity of exploration. Such continuity, in turn, is dependent upon the achievement of an ongoing movement which is consistently controlled by the perceptual stimuli which determine the area to be explored.

Thus movement can be seen as a basic aspect of development and learning in children.[1] Research studies have demonstrated a relationship between such developmental learnings and academic success in public school classrooms.[2] Investigations in classrooms and clinics have shown that special attention to early motor learning can improve school achievement in the primary grades.[3]

---

[1] Frostig, M. *Movement Education: Theory and Practice.* (Chicago: Follett Educational Corporation, 1970).

[2] Ismail, A. H. and Gruber, J. J. *Motor Aptitude and Intellectual Performance.* (Columbus: Chas. E. Merrill, 1967).

[3] Dillon, E. J., Heath, E. J. and Biggs, C. W. *Comprehensive Programming for Success in Learning.* (Columbus: Chas. E. Merrill, 1970).

458456

A large number of children enter the public schools with inadequate or incomplete motor learnings. They are ill-prepared to cope with the responses and manipulative demands placed upon them by classroom tasks. This group of children is variously called "learning disabled," "educationally handicapped," "neurologically impaired," and the like. For this group, the school is required to teach motor competencies of the type which most children bring with them when they begin their school experience.

The obvious center from which such teaching should emanate is the physical education program. This program is devoted to the development of movement and motor skills. However, the competencies required by these children are more than mere motor skills. They are motor generalizations which permit certain types of purposeful exploration and manipulation.[4] Furthermore, the movements must not be isolated and performed for themselves alone. Rather, they must be under continuous perceptual control so that the interaction between the child and his environment, from which learning occurs, can take place.

These additional demands of the slow learning child require an extension and elaboration of the physical education program. Movement patterns must be included which, in the past, have been given little attention. The teaching of skills for the purpose of sports participation and the like must be expanded to include movements for the purpose of exploration and learning. Coordination must be stressed so that the child's attention can shift from how the movement is to be made and can be directed to the interaction which the movement promotes.

Where a specific motor deficit exists, it may be necessary to teach a child on a one-to-one basis using highly specialized exercises of an artificial nature until the defect has been at least partially remediated. Such cases, however, account for a very small part of the total number of children involved. For the vast majority of children (and for the child with the specific defect, as soon as movement is possible), the task is to teach flexible coordinated movement sequences which can serve the child's learning needs. Such teaching can be better accomplished through games and group or individual activities of a more natural and more utilitarian nature.

There is need, therefore, for a series of physical education activities which will aid in the teaching of the basic perceptual-motor

---

[4] Godfrey, B. B. and Kephart, N. C. *Movement Patterns and Motor Education.* (New York: Appleton-Century-Crofts, 1969).

processes which these children have failed to learn. This volume presents such a series. The author has adapted common procedures in physical education to emphasize perceptual-motor learnings and has added new procedures where they seemed needed. Games and group activities are stressed to avoid the artificiality which so often accompanies such training. Although the series is organized around the physical education program, it is not limited to the physical education "class." The classroom teacher will find many suggestions for complementing and augmenting the formal motor program through classroom activities and recreational periods.

The program described herein is designed primarily for special class groups of children all of whom have perceptual-motor problems. However, most of the procedures will be recognized as useful with unsegregated classroom groups as well. For the child in the regular classroom, special attention can be given to his perceptual-motor problem during the course of an activity in which the total group can profitably participate. Thus the usefulness of the program can be greatly expanded beyond the isolated special class situation. All teachers will find many helpful suggestions for aiding the slow learners in their classes.

Newell C. Kephart
Glen Haven Achievement Center
Fort Collins, Colorado

Preface

Physical education has been a significant part of the total educational program for many years. The national trend toward including physical education in the elementary schools recognizes the importance of a wide variety of movement experiences for young children. The value of physical activity as it relates to total fitness is undeniable; an increasing volume of research also indicates the vital role of physical activity in the development of perceptual-motor adequacy.

For some reason, a number of children come to school without the necessary perceptual-motor background to have a successful school experience. This publication is designed to give the classroom teacher, the special teacher and the physical education specialist specific information and instructions in dealing with children with perceptual-motor learning disabilities. However, the teacher will find many of the suggested activities enjoyable and helpful for all youngsters.

Grateful acknowledgement is made to Dr. Newell C. Kephart for his invaluable counsel as the manuscript was being written, and Pam Metz who prepared the drawings. I also wish to acknowledge with gratitude both the pupils and my colleagues within the Denver Public Schools—the former who provided the inspiration for this work and the latter who encouraged me in the labor of writing it.

Robert W. Harvat

To my wife Elizabeth
and our children
Christine
John
Mark

Contents

Specific Activities (continued)

part 1

Generalized Background

A physical activity period, whether it be the informal "recess period" or a highly structured physical education class has been a part of the regular school day for many years. Not only is this an enjoyable period for most children, but the time spent provides the child with the opportunity to develop a degree of physical fitness, physical skills that are highly valued in childhood, and personal-social attitudes. Many teachers maintain that this period is also valuable as an emotional release for boys and girls who sit a major portion of the school day.

Detailed instructional guides and physical education books have been published that outline activity programs to assist teachers. These have been valuable tools especially to those teachers who have had little or no formal training in physical education. These publications are designed to give help to teachers as they deal with "normal" children. Careful child growth and development research, over a period of years, clearly indicates at what grade or age level a particular skill or activity should be introduced. The format of many physical education guides and books has been dependent on this information.

Educators know, however, that children develop at different rates. There are several children in each class who, for one reason or another, do not fall into the "normal" range and consequently have difficulty doing the assigned skill or activity. Some children who have near-

1

FIGURE 1

average or above-average intelligence perform perceptual-motor tasks well below what is considered normal.

Increasingly more research is indicating a strong, positive relationship between the abilities to do perceptual-motor tasks and to achieve academically. The first learnings of the new-born child are motor and this knowledge is foundational to all subsequent learning. From these basic motor activities the child builds a repertoire of motor information about his own body, its movement potential, and its relationship to other objects in his environment. The importance given to this foundation cannot be minimized, for it is the structure upon which more complex learnings are built. A weakness or deficiency in motor development has an effect on perceptual adequacy and later on symbolic and conceptual development. Due to the pyramidal nature of learning, a relatively minor deficiency in motor learning interferes with a larger area of subsequent and more complex learning.

There are several reasons for this interference in learning. The cause of the difficulty may be organic. A neurological defect occurring prior to birth, at birth, or after birth, due to injury or disease, may be the source of the learning problem. The deficiency may arise from a developmental lag. Some children reach readiness stages much later than normally expected. Or, the interference may be caused by persistent emotional stress which restricts essential learning. Finally, some children come to school lacking the necessary background experiences which enable them to perform tasks ordinarily expected of the age group. This experiential or cultural lag may result for several reasons. In our modern society, especially in an urban setting,

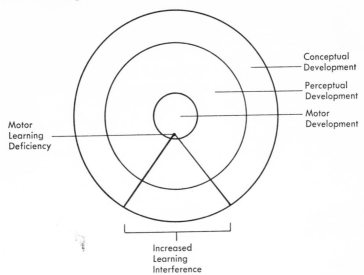

Conceptual Development

Perceptual Development

Motor Development

Motor Learning Deficiency

Increased Learning Interference

FIGURE 2

modern conveniences, automation, television, and the hazards inherent in living today deprive children of essential motor experimentation that is necessary for total development. Overprotective parents may prevent the child from engaging in important developmental experiences. Without question, poverty prohibits some children from engaging in basic experiences. Finally, prolonged or extended illness hinders the normal development in some children.

It becomes apparent that all children should have a multitude of movement experiences. Teachers need not concern themselves with developing in children an exceedingly high proficiency in specific motor skills, but through well-planned programs children establish and strengthen important motor patterns or generalizations. Teachers should give children opportunities to respond through movement to specific instructions within a definite structure. However, equally important is giving children chances to solve meaningful movement problems—to experiment and to discover. Children build a store of knowledge about their own body, its possibilities, and its control (body image). They develop a degree of proficiency in both gross and fine motor coordination and an understanding of laterality, direction, space and time.

To give children the necessary movement experiences the teacher must offer many movement activity alternatives in most physical education periods. If individual needs are to be met, children can no longer be expected to all perform the same activity within a given class period. The teacher must present skills, activities and challenges to highly skilled children in order to keep them motivated and working on tasks in keeping with their abilities. There should be opportunities for others who are not as highly skilled to participate in activities that will lead to the achievement of more complex skills and activities. Appropriate activities for those with perceptual-motor learning disabilities must also be presented. To plan activities to meet the variety of skill and developmental levels within a class is a considerable undertaking, but can be accomplished.

A variety of motor activities must be available, but accompanying these activities must be the type of atmosphere where children feel free to try—where it is all right to make mistakes. Our society places great importance upon physical prowess; prestige is given to those with a high degree of physical skill. In fact, in the elementary school years more prestige among peers is given on the basis of physical ability than upon any other criterion.

Our society also emphasizes competition—who wins or is superior is important. Consequently children need to have an understanding of individual differences, and know that difference in skill is normal. Children must be guided into understanding and empathizing with those who have low motor ability.

When there is a freedom to try, a climate free from criticism and ridicule, the atmosphere will be conducive to real progress for each member of the class.

With a variety of activities geared to meet individual needs, and a warm and supportive atmosphere, teachers, after basic procedures and limitations have been defined, will find that discipline and management problems are kept to a minimum. The rewards and satisfactions for the teacher will be immeasurable.

chapter 1

Teaching the Child with Perceptual-Motor Learning Disabilities

A description of the child with perceptual-motor learning disabilities is very difficult. Often the degree of impairment is the significant factor. The child's disability may be very slight or very severe; he may have only a small number of the symptoms characteristic of these children or he may have a great many.

For ease of presentation and understanding, the characteristics of these children will be listed under four major classifications—academic, physical, emotional and social. A characteristic in one classification, however, may have marked ramifications in others. For example, a common physical trait for children with perceptual-motor learning disabilities is that of hyperactivity. Since the child is so active, he usually is a disruptive member of the class, causing strained social relationships with his peers. Without doubt, continual reprimanding by the teacher over a period of time will cause emotional problems leading to a detrimental effect on the child's feelings about himself. With so many factors interacting, academic success is not possible.

Thus, it must be kept in mind the child is reacting to a complex of factors at any given time.

Academic characteristics. In terms of ability, the child has difficulty with academic tasks, especially reading, spelling, writing, and arithmetic. Although he may express himself exceptionally well verbally, he may have trouble distinguishing left from right, or may reverse numbers and letters often when writing. He may also be confused in determining distance, size, and shape.

A broader problem is that he has difficulty with generalizations and abstractions, and learns best through tangible, concrete, and real experiences. Rules and instructions are easily confused and forgotten; new skills and activities are learned slowly; his ability to understand strategy and make judgments is limited.

Physical characteristics.   The posture and carriage of the child with perceptual-motor learning disabilities appear rigid and inflexible. He is clumsy and awkward, and consequently has difficulty with both gross and fine muscle coordinations.

Since he is hyperactive and highly distractable, concentration on a specific task, even for a short time, becomes a very real problem. In addition, he seems driven by a compulsion to examine objects by touching and handling them.

Equally as perplexing is the child who is hypoactive and withdraws from class activities and new situations.

Emotional characteristics.   He becomes easily frustrated, resulting in explosive or impulsive behavior; temper tantrums are common. Often imaginary illness or aches are used to explain inadequacies or to avoid new situations.

Social characteristics.   As a general rule, peer relationships are poor, causing not only a reluctance to join in class or group activities, but also a rejection of help from his classmates and his teacher.

In a play situation he becomes over-stimulated and does not foresee the results of inappropriate social behavior.

SUCCESSFUL TEACHING METHODS

The teacher who is successful in teaching children, specifically those with perceptual-motor learning disabilities, is one who is sensitive to the problems and needs of these children. He accepts them and their impairment with all the ramifications, thus is patient and willing to spend extra time in planning and working with them. Creativity and resourcefulness are indispensable prerequisites for such teachers.

PLANNING AND PREPARATION

The goal of planning is to prepare tasks where some measure of success is achieved by each child.

In order to provide such activities, it is necessary for the teacher to plan with the children in mind. He should learn as much as possible about each child—his interests, needs, abilities, limitations, past experiences, and the extent of his impairment. A familiarity with the children and a thorough understanding of the subject matter or activities to be presented will allow for a smoother, more meaningful session.

Since transfer of learning from one activity or skill to another will not occur, activities which normal children learn without specific instruction must be taught to these children. Limiting the number of rules or understanding of strategy in each teaching period will provide for more successful activities.

Since these children have difficulty focusing their attention on one activity for a long period of time, short practice sessions with many changes of activity are the most appropriate. Small, step-by-step, concrete presentations utilizing as many senses as possible and overplanning will keep all the children actively participating for the entire period.

Other steps the teacher can take to assure a smoothly run activity period are those involving foresight of possible developments. In attempting to anticipate difficult situations before they occur, the teacher can have alternate plans prepared for circumstances in which his original plans cannot be carried out. If the children are having difficulty, changing the activity or the approach can help assure them a successful experience. All necessary supplies and equipment should be on hand and available before the class arrives. The surroundings should be evaluated and any distracting noise and influences should be reduced as much as possible.

MOTIVATION

When presenting a new activity or maintaining interest in an old one, there are several ways in which a teacher can motivate the children. A story, audio-visual aids of many kinds, or a demonstration by the teacher or another child may serve to keep interest high. The teacher's own enthusiasm is imperative for a motivated class, so again his interest in the class and the activity should be apparent. By changing the name of the activity to one that is more appropriate for an older age level, thus keeping the children in mind and making the activity relevant, the teacher can prevent the class from losing interest in an activity because they think it too young.

PRESENTATION

The teacher can instill a feeling of confidence and friendliness in his class, not only through the tone of his voice, but through the actions and expressions he uses in his presentation. With the children seated and quiet, a calm, well-controlled, but authoritative voice will hold their attention. Directions and instructions should be slow, clear, brief, but thorough.

ACTION

Since the child's success is the teacher's goal, an atmosphere which is relaxed, non-competitive, and free from tension will encourage the child to do his best. Sincere praise for effort and improvement with a minimum of negative statements will help to develop a secure and supportive situation. Mistakes need only be acknowledged as a normal part of living, to be recognized and accepted.

Establish early a definite class organization with well-defined procedures. Not only do children appreciate this structure, but a great deal of time can be conserved. Be consistent and firm when routine procedures are violated and when disciplinary measures are necessary.

If the children work in closely supervised small groups whenever possible, the teacher may find it easier to give enough of the time to learning and practicing new activities and skills. Review and drill on skills can be frequent but enjoyable by using a game approach. A lag in interest should indicate a change in activity, while those activities which remain interesting and lively should be stopped while they are still being enjoyed.

Allowing time at the end of the period to discuss pertinent observations and evaluate class activities can be a useful and valuable teaching technique.

SCHEDULING PHYSICAL ACTIVITY CLASSES

Each school system, depending upon its own particular circumstances, establishes scheduling guidelines that best meet the educational needs of the community. Such factors as finance, available personnel, facilities, established curricular priorities, and the like determine scheduling practices. For instance, in some school systems physical education specialists are employed so that each child has a regularly scheduled physical education period daily. In other situations specialists are used, but they cannot offer a daily program and only particular grade levels, usually older children, have the benefits of a physical education period. Physical education consultants are employed in some communities to conduct inservice programs and advise classroom teachers, who in turn teach the physical activity classes.

Since more importance is being placed on the role of physical education, especially for children in their early years, the trend is to employ physical education specialists. The traditional "recess period" is being replaced with a regularly scheduled, more structured physical activity program. A specific time allotment for physical education is being included as schedules are being developed. Experts agree that a minimum of thirty minutes each day for physical education activities should be established. For some children it is advisable to have additional activity periods.

It is important for classroom teachers, especially primary teachers, to become knowledgeable about perceptual-motor activities. Not only may they be called upon to teach their own physical education class, but also they may supplement and reinforce the activities conducted by the specialist. Many perceptual-motor activities can be conducted in the classroom, and time should be made available in the schedule for this. Some school systems through special education departments have established classes or resource rooms for children who have learning disabilities. Flexible scheduling to meet the needs of individual children is a key consideration. A decision to integrate special classes or individuals within special classes into regular physical education classes must be made by the principal, classroom teachers, and the physical education teacher on the basis of a thorough evaluation. If children from special classes are to be included in regular physical education classes they should be integrated into those groups with children of a similar age level and with a compatible skill performance level. School personnel must keep in mind that children give a great deal of prestige to each other on the basis of physical ability, so that to place children with perceptual-motor deficits into regular physical education classes could add more failures to the many the children have experienced in the past. Therefore, it may be advisable for students in special classes to remain with their own group for the physical activity period until they demonstrate sufficient skill to join those in the regular classes.

It may be necessary for the special class to share the facility with a regular class. Should this occur, grouping children from the two classes together may aid in individualizing the instruction. A detailed explanation is given in the section on grouping. One teacher should not be assigned to a combined regular class and special class.

Generally, in each regular class there are some children who need special help in overcoming perceptual-motor learning disabilities. Instruction can be individualized through flexible scheduling, efficient use of personnel, and careful grouping. In the final analysis, the scheduling of physical education classes in individual buildings depends on circumstances unique to the local situation.

GROUPING FOR EFFICIENT INSTRUCTION

As mentioned earlier, physical education guides and texts have been of great value in advancing sound physical education programs. These publications have been of significant value to teachers as long-range, weekly, and daily plans are developed. Experts in the area of child growth and development have given educators important insights into characteristics, needs, problems and interests that can be expected of children at each age or developmental level. However, it is extremely important that teachers keep in mind that in each classroom there are those who deviate in varying degrees from the "norm." Children develop at vastly different rates. The practice of grouping then takes on great importance.

The benefits derived from grouping children within a regular physical education class which includes some children with perceptual-motor learning disabilities becomes apparent. Through the careful planning of activities for each group, a successful experience can be attained by every child. More efficient use can be made of both the teacher's and children's time. Children can move forward at their own rate of achievement. Oftentimes children with perceptual-motor deficits learn skills and activities more slowly; small groups assure more opportunities to participate and practice in areas of weakness. Since many of these children are highly distractable and have a short attention span, the teacher can change the group activity without interfering with groups of faster moving children. Thus the activities of the more skillful children will not have to be restricted because of those who learn more slowly. After assigning activities the faster moving children are capable of performing, the teacher can give special help to those children with specific weaknesses.

Teachers must take the time to know each child as well as possible. In order to place each child in the appropriate group, he will need to give a variety of tests, to structure his observation, and to read available cumulative and medical records. When assigning children to groups he can consider social traits to place individuals advantageously.

Mobility is an important factor as grouping procedures are being developed. Children should have the opportunity to progress from group to group as skill is attained. Grouping, too, should be flexible from activity to activity. For example, a child having difficulty with mat and rope activities may perform ball activities with a high degree of skill.

As a general rule, most skills and activities will first be presented to the entire class before separating children into individual groups. The number of groups will depend upon the range of skill levels. However, teachers should start with a small number of groups initially and gradually establish more groups as children become more accustomed to this procedure. With some classes, due to classroom control problems, it will not be possible for teachers to establish the number of groups he would like to form. The teacher should expect failure occasionally, but this should not deter him from continuing grouping practices. Many times the failures offer the substance for excellent teaching opportunities.

Teachers should examine the possibility of using highly skilled children to assist those who have specific weaknesses. Communication oftentimes is better between peers than between the teacher and child. However, teachers must exercise care in assigning skilled children to aid those learning more slowly. The helper must not only have the physical skill but also the patience, understanding and empathy to be of benefit to those who are poorly skilled.

More and more use is being made of high school aides, lay aides, and paraprofessionals to assist in individualizing programs. There may be possibilities to use these personnel not only during the regular school day, but also at the noon hour, or before and after school.

Efficient grouping can also take place within the special class. Once the individual needs of each child have been identified, small groups or even individual tasks can be assigned to overcome weaknesses. Again, the use of older children, aides, or paraprofessionals could be of great value. Occasionally the entire class will participate as one unit, but these activities must be as noncompetitive and as enjoyable as possible.

A COOPERATIVE VENTURE

The classroom teacher—either the teacher of a regular class with some children with perceptual-motor learning disabilities or the special education teacher—must join with others to do the most effective job possible for these children. The physical education teacher becomes a partner, not only concerned with the physical aspects of the child's growth, but also with other areas of development. Two or more teachers attempting to be as consistent as possible in instructional practices and classroom management will be far more effective with a particular group than those who do not strive for this consistency. When two or more teachers are working on predetermined objectives, complementing, augmenting and reinforcing each other's teaching, the value to children is immeasurable. The physical education teacher reinforcing basic vocabulary presented in the classroom and the classroom teacher supplementing body image concepts originated in the gymnasium are teaching procedures to be highly recommended.

To attain this cooperation, regularly scheduled meetings of the teaching personnel involved must be arranged. Teachers of a particular class then can pursue such topics as strong and weak areas of each child's development, methods of grouping and individualizing instructions, culminating activities, basic attitudes to be established, preparation of lesson plans in areas of common concern, and evaluation procedures.

In most cases, however, it is extremely difficult for schools to find a regular time or a routine for scheduling frequent joint meetings of teaching personnel. Sometimes other alternatives must be found. Although there should be continuing efforts made for regular and frequent meetings, the following are suggestions for aiding communication between teaching personnel engaged in teaching the same children.

Take advantage of preplanning or mid-year planning sessions, if available. Most school systems provide time in the year for teachers to prepare, organize, plan and to evaluate work within their school.

Occasionally faculty meeting time should be devoted to communication between teachers. The physical education teachers need opportunities to discuss items of concern with the classroom teacher or special education teachers.

An occasional visit by the classroom teacher to the physical education class or visits to the classroom by the physical education teachers may offer new perspectives for the visiting teacher. Not only is there an opportunity for the teacher to see children operate in a different situation, but it offers an occasion to observe the teaching techniques of the other teacher.

Conscientious teachers are constantly exploring ways in which they can work together to be of greater help to children. It is obvious that often a great deal of time over and above that normally expected of teachers must be devoted to accomplish the objectives established for the class.

PARAPROFESSIONALS—AIDES

Increasingly, school systems are hiring paraprofessionals and aides. The primary purpose for employing this personnel is to free the teacher so he can spend maximum time with children on direct instruction and planning. Paraprofessionals and aides take over such time-consuming activities as: readying equipment and supplies; collecting lunch money and fees; clerical and secretarial work; bulletin boards, cafeteria, hall, and playground supervision; and like activities.

Paraprofessionals and aides with proper training can be utilized to supervise or instruct individual children or small groups in areas of weakness. They can free the teacher from the supervision of a large group, self-directed activity, allowing him to give specialized help to a child or children with specific needs.

Not only should paraprofessionals and aides be given adequate training in specific techniques, but they should be screened carefully to be certain they have the necessary personal qualities to be of service to these children.

STUDENT ASSISTANCE

Student assistance can be divided into the following three classifications; the college or university student contemplating entrance into the teaching professions, the high school students, and the older students within the school.

Early in his preparation the college or university student who plans to make teaching his career should have many exposures to actual teaching situations, before being thrust into the usual student teaching program in the final year. These teaching situations, as a part of regular course work, would allow students to instruct individuals or small groups. Any work with children obviously would be preceded with appropriate training. Students interested in or specializing in physical education can be given assignments to assist children having difficulty with perceptual-motor tasks. Later, students may wish to specialize in the area of adaptive physical education or special education. At any rate, this experience can be of mutual benefit to the teacher in preparation and to the children that can be given special help.

A practice becoming more prevalent is the utilization of high school students as aides in elementary schools. These students, helping out for various reasons (service projects, examination of career opportunities, etc.), are proving to be a valuable asset to the schools. Not only do they relieve the teacher of routine duties, but often the high school student is capable of communicating an idea or a concept more easily and more effectively than the regular teacher. Again, these students must be screened carefully and given the appropriate training.

The possibilities of assigning older elementary pupils to lower grades within the same school should be examined. Older students, due to the admiration given by younger children, could have a significant impact on their learning. After some basic instruction these children would be especially valuable in assisting primary children with some fundamental physical skills and activities. Uninhibited communication between these children, both vocal and demonstrative, could be one of the most effective teaching techniques available. Again, as with other aides, careful screening is a necessity. Teachers who do this screening should not only look for children who have the understanding, empathy and patience, but also those who could use this ego-building experience.

chapter 2

Identification and Evaluation

The observant teacher rather quickly picks out those children having difficulty with motor tasks. Often, however, teachers only evaluate in general terms—he is very clumsy, he learns skills very slowly and with great difficulty, he does not participate or he avoids activity by bothering others. It is apparent that before individual needs can be met some identifying techniques are necessary.

Usually, teachers do not have the time necessary to do a great deal of formal testing, but before they can be efficient, they need an indicator of weak areas for children having difficulty.

There are several ways teachers can organize their classes in order to utilize some identifying techniques.

1. If the teacher is by himself, he can engage the class in a familiar activity while he selects a few children to test.
2. Most of the identifying activities are a part of the regular program. For example, if the children are participating in gymnastics, the teacher may test as many as possible on the balance beam while the remainder of the class participates in tumbling, rope activities, or on other apparatus. If the children are participating in ball skill activities, the teachers may go to each small group and quickly test each member.
3. During an exercise warm up time at the beginning of the period, the teacher may focus his attention on a few children he suspects are having difficulty.

4. In some situations two or more teachers may work together; one teacher tests a small number while the other teacher(s) supervises the remainder of the class.
5. Aides and paraprofessionals may be trained to do the testing or they may supervise the classes and release the teacher to do the testing.

Each teacher, on the basis of his schedule and the local situation, should determine the best time to employ identifying techniques.

The physical education teacher, the classroom teacher and/or others who contact members of the same class should arrange conferences to compare observations and tests of individual children.

The following identifying techniques can be conducted in either of two ways. 1. Tests are given as a particular seasonal or activity unit is introduced. For example, during the gymnastic activities the balance beam test can be given. During rhythmic activities the jump, hop, and skip can be tested. 2. All tests can be scheduled early in the year. Arrangements can be made for retests throughout the year.

ANGELS IN THE SNOW

The child is on his back, arms at his sides, feet together. Prepare him by having him move his arms upward, keeping the elbows straight, until his hands touch over the head. Return to the starting position. Have the child move his legs apart as far as possible, knees stiff. Return. Remind the child when the arms move they must remain in contact with the floor and when the legs move, the heels must remain in contact with the floor. The teacher should point to the arms or legs to be moved. Have the child do the following:

1. Move the right arm overhead. Return to starting position.
2. Repeat using left arm.
3. Move the right leg to side. Return.
4. Repeat using the left leg.
5. Move both arms overhead. Return.
6. Move both legs to side. Return.
7. Move both arms and both legs. Return.
8. Move right arm and right leg. Return.
9. Move left arm and left leg. Return.
10. Move right arm and left leg. Return.
11. Move left arm and right leg. Return.

Observe:

1. freedom of action (rigidity, hesitancy)
2. ease in identifying limb(s) to be moved
3. overflow movement into other body parts
4. inability to perform
5. no attempt

JUMP

The child springs one jump forward, backward, sideward right and sideward left. Instruct the child to keep his feet together.
Observe:

1. freedom of action (rigidity, hesitancy)
2. maintenance of balance on landing
3. both feet leaving floor simultaneously
4. inability to perform
5. no attempt

HOP

The child hops in place using the following patterns:

1. Hop on the right foot. (Continue until signal to stop.)
2. Repeat using the left foot.
3. Hop twice on the right foot and twice on the left foot. (Continue until the signal to stop.)
4. Hop once on the right foot and once on the left foot. (Continue until the signal to stop.)
5. Hop twice on the right foot and once on the left foot. (Continue until the signal to stop.)
6. Hop twice on the left foot and once on the right foot. (Continue until the signal to stop.)

Observe:

1. freedom of action (rigidity, hesitancy)
2. ease in shifting body weight
3. continuity of rhythm
4. inability to perform
5. no attempt

SKIP

The child skips continuously in a given space.
Observe:

1. freedom of action (rigidity, hesitancy)
2. continuity of rhythm
3. inability to perform
4. no attempt

Older children should be asked to perform more difficult steps or patterns. For example, a step-hop; a two step (step close step); a basic schottische step (step, step, step, hop); or a bleking step (jump with right heel forward—hold, jump with left heel forward—hold, jump right, left, right, in quick time, hold).

BALANCE

The child walks a four inch wide balance beam forward, backward, sideward (both right and left).
Observe:

1. freedom of action (rigidity, hesitancy)
2. difficulty maintaining balance (stepping off more than once or twice on each crossing)
3. avoid balancing by moving too fast
4. inability to perform
5. no attempt

BEAN BAG ACCURACY

The children attempt to toss a bean bag into a box or waste-basket. Allow three throws. Distance will vary with age level.
Observe:

1. freedom of action (rigidity)
2. accuracy
3. type of throw (both hands, one hand, overhand, under-hand)
4. inability to perform
5. no attempt

CATCH AND THROW (8½″ UTILITY BALL)

Throw the ball to the child so that it bounces once. Repeat two more times.
Observe:

1. freedom of action (fear reaction, rigidity)
2. timing
3. inability to perform
4. no attempt

The teacher may increase the distance and/or remove the bounce when testing older children.
The child throws the ball three times.
Observe:

1. freedom of action (rigidity)
2. accuracy (distance and direction)
3. type of throw (both hands, one hand, overhand, under-hand)
4. inability to perform
5. no attempt

BALL BOUNCE

The child bounces the ball five times using both hands. Repeat using the right hand and left hand. The child bounces the ball ten times using alternate hands.
Observe:

1. freedom of action (rigidity)
2. timing and rhythm
3. inability to perform
4. no attempt

Evaluations conducted in the regular physical education classes may give additional data which will assist in identifying children with perceptual-motor learning disabilities. For example, the sit-up, pull-up, push-up, and standing long jump tests may supplement or reinforce information being gathered about individual children. Likewise, skill tests, such as ball throw for distance, place kick for distance, punt for distance, soccer dribble, volleyball serve, softball pitch for accuracy, high jump or running long jump add to the data being accumulated about each child. The regular gymnastic program and the rhythm program afford another excellent opportunity to observe children.

In all probability the physical activity period is the most informal part of the school day. Since this is true, teachers see children in a freer situation. Other aspects of development can be studied, such as:

peer relations
attention span
hypoactivity-hyperactivity
distractibility
self-control
self-confidence
reaction to success or failure
reaction to new and different activities
effort
honesty
adherence to regulations and rules

PERCEPTUAL-MOTOR EVALUATION

The evaluation form is a screening device used not only to discover specific weaknesses in individual children, but also can be used as a total evaluation of physical education performance. Some suggested uses are as follows, but in its final analysis each teacher will determine its best use.

1. Administer the entire test early in the school year to each child in the class.
2. Those children performing well on all tests need no retesting until the following year.
3. Those children having specific problems, after participating in a specially designed program, will be retested at a later date in areas of weakness.
4. Some children with severe difficulties should be tested in all areas one or more times during the year.

Some teachers may choose to use the evaluation form on a seasonal basis in connection with physical fitness testing and skill testing. The Angels in the Snow Test can be administered as a part of the physical fitness testing program. The Balance Test can be used during a gymnastic unit. The Bean Bag and Ball Tests can be done during seasonal ball activities.

INSTRUCTION FOR USING PERCEPTUAL-MOTOR EVALUATION

1. Fill in the spaces for name, age, grade and room number.
2. Record the date (there is space for four test and retest sessions.
3. Know how to administer each test—know what to look for.
4. Study the key. (The tester, after evaluating several children, will become proficient.)
5. Record pertinent comments whenever necessary. Comments should give the tester an indication of what to look for when retesting. For example, on the Jump Test an appropriate comment would be: "unable to keep feet together" or on the Catch and Throw Test, "unable to judge speed of approaching ball." Comments of a positive nature should also be recorded.
6. Record performance on physical fitness tests or skill tests.
7. Note, as objectively as possible, personal qualities, such as aggressiveness, withdrawal, cooperation. Also comment on peer relationships, reaction to authority, and the like.

PERCEPTUAL-MOTOR EVALUATION

Key

1. Excellent Performance **2.** Good (only minor problems) **3.** Mediocre (needs participation in similar activities)
4. Marked Difficulty (needs special help) **5.** Serious problems (refer)

Name_____ Age___ Grade___ Room___

Dates_____

1. Angels in the Snow

   Bilateral   _____ _____ _____
   Unilateral   _____ _____ _____
   Cross-lateral _____ _____ _____
   Comments:

2. Jump

   forward   _____ _____ _____
   backward   _____ _____ _____
   sideward right _____ _____ _____
   sideward left _____ _____ _____

   Comments:

3. Hop

   even patterns (one right), (one left), (two right—
   two left), etc. _____ _____ _____
   uneven patterns (two right—one left), (two left—one
   right) _____ _____ _____

   Comments:

4. Skip

   (step-hop, two step, schottische,
   bleking) _____ _____ _____

   Comments:

5. Balance (Balance Beam)

   forward   _____ _____ _____
   backward   _____ _____ _____
   sideward right _____ _____ _____
   sideward left _____ _____ _____

   Comments:

6. Bean Bag Accuracy

   _____ _____ _____

   Comments:

7. Catch and Throw

   catch _____ _____ _____
   throw _____ _____ _____

   Comments:

8. Ball Bounce

   both hands _____ _____ _____
   right hand _____ _____ _____
   left hand _____ _____ _____
   alternate hands _____ _____ _____

   Comments:

9. Other Physical Fitness or Skill Tests

   _____ _____ _____ _____ _____ _____ _____ _____ _____
   _____ _____ _____ _____ _____ _____ _____ _____ _____
   _____ _____ _____ _____ _____ _____ _____ _____ _____
   _____ _____ _____ _____ _____ _____ _____ _____ _____

10. General Comments, Personal—Social

part 2

Specific Activities

The activity sections which follow give specific instructions and suggestions to teachers for a wide variety of physical activities as they plan programs for children with perceptual-motor learning problems. Since these activities are suitable, profitable, and enjoyable for all children, they should be included in the program for the entire class. The suggested activities are basic, so teachers will probably wish to add, modify, and experiment with many more.

Since the emphasis should be on individualizing as much as possible, the activities have not been assigned a grade level. The teacher, after discovering the capabilities and limitations of each child, should plan and present an activity program based on identified needs. Teachers of older children may find it necessary to begin activity sequences that are very basic. If the activities are considered too childish, a great deal of ingenuity will be necessary to stimulate these children to participate.

The activities in each section are listed in a suggested order of difficulty from simple to more difficult. It will be necessary for some children to start at the beginning of a particular sequence, while others at a more advanced level can begin with more complex activities. Others, because of a high degree of proficiency, can completely by-pass some activity progressions.

Teachers are encouraged to plan daily lessons utilizing activities from various sections, not presenting all the activities in one section before going to the next.

Fundamental Locomotor Movements

FIGURE 3

The basic locomotor activities can be very beneficial because they aid children in building a better understanding of body image and assist in developing neuromuscular control, laterality, directionality, balance and rhythm.

To assist in the development of rhythm as fundamental locomotor activities are being practiced, the teacher may ask some children to accompany the movements with rhythm instruments, whether they be commercially prepared or constructed of readily accessible materials; e.g., coffee cans, wastebaskets, plastic jugs, sandpaper blocks or paired sticks made from broom handles. Children can also perform locomotor movements to a rhythm set by clapping their hands, tapping their hands and feet or moving to phonograph records.

Whenever possible, have children do the fundamental movement *in place* before moving about. Add another dimension by having children verbalize their movements, for example, have them say *step, step, step* or *slide, slide, slide* or *jump, jump, jump* as they do the prescribed activity.

As skills improve, children can participate with a partner or in a small group where they practice matching steps with others.

The following activities offer some basic suggestions; the possibilities are unlimited. The teacher should plan activities and combinations of activities in keeping with the abilities and needs of the group.

ACTIVITIES INVOLVING WALKING

Walk forward, backward, and sideward, both left and right.
Vary the speed from a normal walk to a fast walk or a slow walk.
Vary the height and length of the steps.
Change the intensity of the step—light, heavy, tiptoe or march.
Walk forward, backward, or sideward, touching the left hand to the left knee and the right hand to the right knee as each step is taken.
Walk forward, backward, or sideward, touching the left knee with the right hand and the right knee with the left hand.
Walk with the feet crossing the body's midline. Use a line as a guide to step across. Vary by having the hand of the same side or the opposite side accompany the foot across the midline.
Use a combination of walking steps. For example, have the children tiptoe three steps, walk three steps, stamp three steps; or take four long steps and four short steps; or take six fast-short steps and six slow-high steps; or walk with one foot and stamp (or tiptoe) with the other.

ACTIVITIES INVOLVING RUNNING

Run forward and backward.
Vary the speed of the running step, fast or slow.
Vary the height and length of the running step.
Change the intensity of the step—light or heavy.
Bring knees up to a prancing step.
Use a combination of running steps. For example, run to the wall using short, light steps and return by running backward using slow, heavy steps; or alternate a series of high-light tiptoeing steps with a series of low-heavy steps; or run in a crouched position gradually coming to an upright position running lightly on tiptoes, arms extended over head.

ACTIVITIES INVOLVING JUMPING

Jump forward, backward, and sideward, both left and right.
Vary the speed of the jump, fast or slow.

Vary the height and length of the jump.
Change the intensity of the jump—light or heavy.
Jump as high as possible from a crouched position.
Jump and land on one foot (alternate).
Use a combination of jumping activities. For example, take four quick, light jumps forward and four slow, heavy jumps backward; or take three jumps gradually moving the feet to a stride position and three jumps gradually moving feet to original position; or take three slow jumps to the right and three fast jumps to the left.

ACTIVITIES INVOLVING HOPPING

Hop forward and backward. Use both the right foot and the left foot.
Hop sideward, moving right using the right foot; left using the left foot; left using the right foot; right using the left foot.
Vary the speed of the hop, fast or slow.
Vary the height and length of the hop.
Change the intensity of the hop—light or heavy.
Hop from one foot landing on two feet (alternate feet).
Take two hops and hold balance.
Take a long hop and hold balance.
Use a combination of hopping activities. For example, do a series of rapid hops on one foot and a series of slow hops on the other foot (alternate); or do a series of long, heavy hops on one foot and a series of high, light hops on the other foot (alternate); or alternate six hops on the right foot with six hops on the left foot, then four hops right, four hops left, two hops right, two hops left, and one hop right, one hop left; or hop three times on right, two on left and continue; or hop three times on left and one time on right and continue; or hop one time on right, and two times on left, and continue.
The hop offers an unlimited number of combination possibilities. The teacher should plan activities moving from simple ones to more complex combinations.

ACTIVITIES INVOLVING SKIPPING

Skip forward and backward.
Vary the speed of the skip—fast or slow.
Vary the height and length of the skip.

Change the intensity of the skip—light or heavy.

Use a combination of skipping activities. For example, do a series of quick skips forward and a series of slow skips backward; or move with short, light skips gradually changing to long, heavy skips.

Since a great deal of enjoyment and prestige is derived from skipping, special consideration should be given to those children having difficulty. When teaching the skip start first with the hop. Have the children take several hops on the right foot and then on the left. Reduce the number of hops being done on each foot until they are alternating one hop on the right foot and one hop on the left foot. Gradually increase the speed of this very slow step-hop until they are skipping.

Another more mechanical approach is to have the children step on one foot and hop on it, step on the other foot and hop on it, again, gradually increasing the speed. It may be valuable for some children to have the teacher point to or touch the foot on which the hopping should be done.

ACTIVITIES INVOLVING GALLOPING

Gallop forward and backward, alternating the lead foot.
Vary the speed of the gallop, fast or slow.
Vary the height and length of the gallop.
Change the intensity of the gallop—light or heavy.
Use a combination of galloping activities. For example, take six gallops backward using the left foot as the lead foot; or do a series of high gallops followed by a series of low gallops; or gallop using slow, heavy movements gradually increasing the speed to fast, light movements; or gallop seven times with the right foot leading, gallop seven times with the left foot leading, continue five right, five left—three right, three left—two right, two left—one right, one left.

ACTIVITIES INVOLVING SLIDING

Slide right and left.
Vary the speed of the slide, fast or slow.
Vary the height or length of the slide.
Change the intensity of the slide—light or heavy.
Use a combination of sliding activities. For example, slide to the

right using a slow, heavy slide and return using a fast, light slide (alternate); or take long slides left and high slides right (alternate).

ACTIVITIES COMBINING FUNDAMENTAL LOCOMOTOR MOVEMENTS

Teachers will wish to add many more combinations to the following examples:

Walk forward four steps; take four jumps backward.

Do eight skips; take eight gallops, right foot leading; take eight gallops, left foot leading.

Walk four steps; take eight skips.

Take four jumps; do four hops left; four hops right; walk six steps.

Add the elements of speed, direction and intensity to the combinations.

The concept of form often is difficult for some children having perceptual-motor learning disabilities. Teachers can use chairs, Indian clubs, or floor-marking tape placed in the shape of a triangle, square, rectangle, diamond, etc. and have the children move from one object to the other using one of the basic movements, thus aiding or reinforcing an understanding of simple geometric forms. For example:

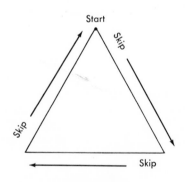

FIGURE 4

As children become more skillful, involve more of the basic movements as in Figure 5.

The more difficult combinations will necessitate memorizing the method of travel between objects, again attacking a common problem of many of these children. The teacher should begin with easy combinations and progress to more complex ones as memory and skill improve.

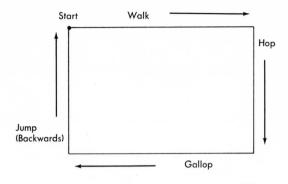

FIGURE 5

Exercises

FIGURE 6

A large number of children with perceptual-motor learning disabilities have consistently met with failure in many physical activities. Since they are unsuccessful, these children have avoided vigorous activity and consequently lack the physical strength, flexibility, endurance and agility to do many of the tasks normally expected of them. Teachers must begin an exercise program slowly, gradually increasing the number of exercises and the repetitions of each.

Not only can a well-planned and conducted program of exercises aid the physical fitness of children, but it can also assist in overcoming specific difficulties—problems with spacial relationships, laterality, directionality, coordination and body image.

Teachers should plan a sequence of activities utilizing a variety of exercises for each session. Since exercise activities are somewhat mechanical, children may lose interest quickly. Thus, using the entire activity period for exercise should be avoided. When engaging in exercises, children should be motivated to do each one with enthusiasm and vigor.

The activities that are listed in this section are primarily gross motor exercises, and should serve only as a starting point. Teachers will want to add variations to the ones described and use many other exercises.

BEAR HUG

From a standing position, have the children take a long step diagonally forward with the right foot and tightly encircle the thigh with both arms. They should then return to the starting position and repeat stepping forward on the left foot.

KNEE LIFT

From a standing position, the children lift their right knees and grasp them with both hands pulling them tightly to their chests. Return to the starting position. Repeat lifting left knees. Have children do this exercise slowly to involve balance.

WINDMILL

The children stand in a stride position, knees straight, bending at the waist; right hands up and left hands down, elbows straight. Then alternately touch the right hands to the left toes and the left hands to the right toes. Vary the speed.

HEAD ROLL

The children slowly rotate their heads to the right or to the left. Have them move their heads forward, backward, right and left.

TRUNK BEND

The children stand, feet slightly apart, arms overhead, and bend as far as possible to the right, left, forward or backward. Have them rotate to the right or left. Children can vary this exercise by doing it sitting or kneeling.

JUMPING JACK

From a standing position, arms at the sides, children jump to a stride position and simultaneously clap the hands overhead keeping the elbows straight. They then return to the starting position. It is important to maintain a consistent rhythm. Have the children use the following variations with the arms as legs move apart and together:

Start with hands on shoulders, extend arms to side and return to shoulders.

Start with arms extended to the side, flex elbows bringing hands to shoulders, return to the extended position.

Start with hands on shoulders, extend arms forward and return to shoulders.

Start with arms extended forward, flex elbows bringing hands to shoulders, return to extended position.

Start with hands on shoulder, extend arms overhead and return to shoulders.

Start with arms extended overhead, flex elbows bringing hand to shoulders, return to extended position.

Start with the right arm at side and the left extended overhead, move right arm overhead as the left moves to the side. Return to starting position.

Turn the head to right or left as the legs go apart.

BACK INCLINE

The children sit, legs extended in front, hands beside the hips, palms down. Have them raise the body to an inclined position putting all the weight on the hands and ankles. They then return to a sitting position. They can vary this exercise by raising or flexing one leg as the hips are lifted from the floor (alternate).

SUPINE ACTION

The children assume a position on their backs, legs straight, hands at sides, palms down. They raise the legs approximately ten inches off the floor and hold for about three seconds. Other variations are as follows:

Raise the right and left leg independently.

Lift both legs to right angles, the right leg and left leg independently.

Flex both knees and bring to the chest, the right knee and the left knee independently.

With the legs resting on the floor, flex and extend both feet, the right foot and the left foot independently, or rotate both feet on the heels, the right foot and left foot independently.

From the supine position, arms extended over head, have the

children sit up reaching forward with extended arms. At the same time they bring the knees to the chest, the arms on the outside of the knees. They then return to starting position. Vary this exercise by doing the following:

Sit up, reaching with the left arm and flexing the left knee. Repeat on right side.
Sit up, reaching with left arm and flexing right knee.
Repeat using opposite extremities.

TOE TOUCH

The children sit, legs together and extended in front. They reach forward and touch toes, holding this position for three seconds. Those having difficulty should first touch the shins, then the ankles. This exercise can also be done while standing.

SIT-UP

Each child has a partner. The exerciser lies on his back, arms extended over head, legs straight, feet together, while his partner holds his ankles. The exerciser comes to a sitting position and should do the following each time the sitting position is attained:

Touch the right shin with both hands, then the left shin.
Alternately touch the right shin with the right hand and the left shin with the left hand.
Touch the right shin with the left hand, the left shin with the right hand.

The child changes the original position by flexing his knees and placing feet flat on floor. He laces his fingers behind his head, and his partner now holds the insteps. He then does the sequence listed above with the elbows touching the knees. He sits up by first lifting the head, then the neck and shoulders and finally the rest of the upper body.

BICYCLE

Children assume a position on their backs; they roll back on the neck and shoulders, place the hands on the hips. The weight is supported on the elbows, neck and shoulders. The feet revolve alternately as in bicycle riding.

PRONE ACTION

Have the children lie on their stomachs, keeping the knees straight, and lifting the legs as high as possible. They can vary this exercise by doing the following:

Lift the right and left leg independently.
Flex the knees, bring both feet to the buttocks. Flex the right and left knee independently.
Lace the fingers behind the head and raise the upper body as high as possible. Hold for three seconds.
Raise both upper body and legs, keeping the knees straight.
Raise upper body and legs and rock back and forth.

PUSH-UP

From a position on the stomach, have children place their hands under the shoulders, fingers forward. They push up keeping the body in a straight line from the toes to the head. Have them return, touching the chest or chin to the floor. Children having difficulty should do push-ups with knees remaining on the floor.

WING STRETCHER

The children raise their elbows to the side to about shoulder level, and force elbows backward vigorously. They then return to the original position. This exercise can be done standing, kneeling or sitting.

ARM CIRCLES (PROPELLERS)

The children raise extended arms sideward to about shoulder level. They rotate their arms forward, backward, palms up and down. They can vary this exercise by doing the following:

Change the speed of the action.
Vary the size of the circles.

Raise the arms forward to shoulder level, and rotate the right arm counterclockwise as the left arm rotates clockwise. Rotate right arm clockwise as the left arm rotates counterclockwise. Circle both arms in a clockwise direction. Circle both arms counterclockwise. Repeat this exercise with the arms either over head or angled downward at a 45 degree angle.

Repeat these exercises while the children are lying on their backs using their legs.

FIST CLENCHER

Children raise their arms to the side, elbows straight, and open and close the hands forcibly. They should do this exercise with the arms extended to the front or overhead.

THUMB TOUCH

The children touch each finger in turn with the thumb of the same hand. Have them do this exercise with both hands simultaneously or with each hand independently.

CHANGE POSITION

From a sitting position on the floor, knees flexed, feet in front, children move to a standing position and return to sitting position. They can vary this exercise by doing it from a sitting position with the legs crossed; or from a kneeling position.

From a position on the back, children stand by rolling forward.

From a position on the stomach, children place hands on floor and jump to a standing position.

ISOLATE THE PART

Children move the part of the body indicated without affecting any other part. For example, they bend the right knee, or extend the left arm, or swing the left leg, or rotate the right wrist.

SQUAT THRUST

From a standing position, children squat placing their hands on the floor outside of the knees. The legs are thrust backward so that the body is straight from shoulders to feet (push-up position). They return to squat position; stand.

ROCKER

The children stand, bend at the waist and touch the toes without bending the knees. They flex the knees, raising the extended arms parallel to the floor. Have them return to toe touch position; stand.

ANGELS IN THE SNOW

Review this exercise. (See page 16.) Vary by doing this activity on the stomach, or sitting on the floor with the legs in front and the knees together, or standing.

Game Activities

FIGURE 7

Game activities play a very important role in the physical activity period. Not only do they provide an enjoyable and vigorous activity, but they can also allow an emotional release that is vital. Through careful observation, teachers have opportunities to see social relationships and can structure the class in such a way as to benefit many children. Games also provide opportunities for the teacher to discover and assist those children with perceptual-motor problems.

Most games can be adapted or modified to meet particular needs. For example, instead of always having children run around the circle or to a base, vary the mode of travel—skip, hop, jump, gallop, etc. When appropriate and safe, have children move sidewards or backwards. In games that involve touching or tagging others, have children tag only with the right hand or only with the left hand, or by tossing a bean bag or a light plastic ball at other players. Since there are many excellent physical education activity books available to teachers (see Bibliography), this game activity section is short and incomplete. The games included are examples of some that can be valuable in developing an awareness of body image, assist with laterality, directionality, balance, and aid motor control.

FOLLOW THE LEADER

The teacher appoints one child to be the leader, and has the remainder of the group form a single line behind him. The followers must duplicate each action done by the leader. It is important that the leader keeps the line moving and uses many different, interesting tasks. The leader should use a variety of locomotor movements, animal walks, and stunts. The teacher encourages movements that involve changes in speed, intensity, posture and direction. Several groups should be formed when the group is large.

HOW CAN WE GET THERE?

Two parallel boundaries are drawn about 20 yards apart. Each boundary line is given the name of a large city. All of the children move to one line. A child is selected to tell how he could get to the "other city." He may say, "jump," in which case all must jump to the other line. Then a new leader is selected. Each leader must choose a different way of traveling between lines, and may not repeat a way of moving previously used.

ONE, TWO, WHAT CAN YOU DO?

The children form a single circle. One child is selected to be in the middle. He spins around with his eyes closed, pointing with his finger. As he spins he says, "One, two, what can you do?" and stops on the word "do." The player at whom he is pointing must answer, "I can hop (or skip or crabwalk or push-up)."

The center player then says, "If he can do it, so can we, get ready to go when I count three—one, two, three." On *three* everyone performs the specified activity. The player choosing the activity becomes the new center person; the first center player returns to the circle. Teachers may wish to add the rule that an activity may only be used once.

DO THIS, DO THAT

This game is not only enjoyable for children, but also may be a valuable aid to the teacher in identifying children with perceptual-motor learning disabilities.

The children stand facing the leader. The leader changes the position of his body or moves any part of his body and says, "Do this." Immediately, the others assume the same position. If the leader changes position and says "Do that," any player copying the action must be seated. The object is to see which children can remain standing for the longest time. However, the teacher should find ways to quickly include those who have been eliminated in order to maintain interest and to assist those children having difficulty. It may be necessary, at times, to help some children decide that they have been eliminated. While playing *Do This, Do That* have children imitate the following arm movements:

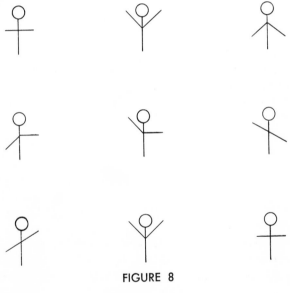

FIGURE 8

SIMON SAYS

The children stand facing the leader. The leader gives various commands involving body movement. The leader obeys all of his commands, but other players comply only when the commands are preceded by the words "Simon Says." For example, the leader calls, "Simon says, touch your toes" and executes the command himself.

All other players should quickly comply. If the leader calls "Squat down" (the leader obeys) the others should not move. Those who err are eliminated. Once again, the teacher should find ways to quickly include these children. For example, the first children caught move to a designated corner or location in the room, then move to a second location when the next children who are caught move to the first location. The first ones eliminated may return to the game when the third player or group of players are eliminated. Thus, there is a continued rotation.

This game also can be used as a way of identifying children with perceptual-motor learning disabilities. Some children have difficulty locating and identifying body parts. As children are participating in the game the following commands can be given: touch your eyes; touch your ears; touch your shoulders; touch your nose; touch your ankles; touch your elbows; etc.

BUSY BEE

After selecting a leader, match each child with a partner. Partners follow the directions called out by the leader, for example: hands to hands; elbows to elbows; toes to toes; back to back; face to face; etc. When the leader calls "Busy Bee," he quickly gets a partner as everyone attempts to find a new partner. The one without a partner becomes the new leader.

TANGLE TAG

One child is selected to be "it." The remainder of the children run at random until "it" calls "tangle." At this time the players balance on one foot, place an arm under the raised leg, and grasp the nose. "It" can tag a player before he grasps his nose or if he loses his balance and releases his nose. The player tagged is the new "It."

Jump Rope Activities

FIGURE 9

The challenge of jumping rope fills much leisure time of children at some point in their elementary school years. Since jumping rope has been a traditional school activity, many teachers make ropes available and assume that children will be successful with very little specific instruction. For many children this is not the case. A definite step-by-step teaching sequence is essential.

Jump rope activities are valuable for these children because they involve a coordination of the feet, hands, and eyes. These activities are beneficial in developing spacial relationships and a sense of rhythm or timing.

Before actually involving ropes, the teacher should review many of the hopping and jumping activities listed in the section on Fundamental Locomotor Movements.

ACTIVITIES INVOLVING ONE LONG ROPE
(12 FT. TO 15 FT.)

After stretching the rope straight on the floor, have children follow these movements:

Jump or hop over the rope both forward and backward.
Zigzag jump, both forward and backward, the length of the rope.

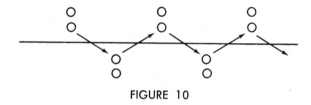

FIGURE 10

Zigzag hop, forward and backward, the length of the rope (right and left foot).

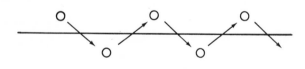

FIGURE 11

Teach the children to land lightly on the balls of the feet. At first, allow children to pause between jumps or hops, then gradually increase the speed.

ACTIVITIES INVOLVING TWO LONG ROPES

Place the ropes on the floor parallel and approximately one foot apart.

Starting outside of the ropes jump or hop between the ropes and out, moving both forward and backward.

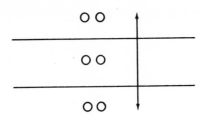

FIGURE 12

Zigzag jump the length of the ropes moving both forward and backward.

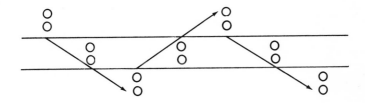

FIGURE 13

Zigzag hop, forward and backward, the length of the ropes (right and left feet).

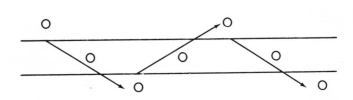

FIGURE 14

Scissors jump, both forward and backward, the length of the ropes.

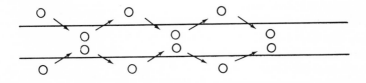

FIGURE 15

ACTIVITIES INVOLVED IN JUMPING A LONG ROPE

One of the first activities involving a moving rope should be *Jump the Shoe (Shot)*.

Tie an old gymnasium shoe or a soft object similar in weight and size to a rope about eight feet in length. The children form a single circle and one is selected to be a turner. The turner swings the rope in a circular fashion so the heavy end brushes the surface of the ground. As the rope rotates, each player attempts to jump the rope. The turner may vary the speed of the swing to confuse the players. Any player not jumping over the rope may either become the new turner or must stay out of the game until another participant has been put out.

Before teaching the skills involved in rope jumping, demonstrate the proper way to turn the rope. Rope turners should stand close enough together to allow two or three feet of rope to hit the ground on each turn. Children should practice using the whole arm when turning a long rope.

Allow children an opportunity to listen to the rhythm of the rope as it turns. Children can mimic this timing without actually attempting to jump the rope. Have them say "jump-bounce" in rhythm with the turning rope. On the word "jump," the children jump with both feet together about three to four inches from the ground; on the word "bounce," they take a very small bounce in place. The child can practice the "jump-bounce" as the rope is swung from side to side, but not over the head. When the jumper is ready, have him stand in and jump the rope, this time with the rope swung over the head.

Next, teach the children to run in and jump an already turning rope. They should practice running in and jumping both when the arc of the rope approaches from the top of the turn and when it approaches from the bottom.

When the arc approaches the jumper from the top of the turn (front door), have him start his run as the rope hits the ground in front of him. The jumper says, "ready, ready, go" as the rope hits the ground three times. This not only establishes the rhythm, but tells the jumper when to start.

When the arc of the rope approaches the jumper from the bottom of the turn (back door), he starts his run when the rope is at the top of the swing. The jumper says "ready, ready, go" as the rope reaches its highest point three times. He must jump the rope as he runs in.

The jumper will need practice in running out of the turning rope without being hit. This can be accomplished by jumping and leaning in the direction he wishes to exit and moving quickly in that direction as he takes his final jump.

As children become more skilled have them run in, drop an object, retrieve it and run out; or run in, bounce or toss up a ball, catch it and run out; or run in and jump an individual rope each time the long rope turns.

ACTIVITIES INVOLVED IN JUMPING A SHORT ROPE (6 FT. TO 8 FT.)

Now the child must turn his own rope. Again, he can practice the "jump-bounce" and pretend to turn the rope. When he can turn the rope and jump with both feet together adequately, add the following: hop on one foot, left and right; jump with the right foot forward or with the left foot forward; skip. Set patterns to be jumped; for example, jump right, left, right, or right, right, left, or left, left, left, right, etc.

To add variety as children become more skillful, have them eliminate the "bounce" or rebound and jump on each turn of the rope. Now the rope must be turned faster.

Balancing Activities

FIGURE 16

Balancing is a skill that causes a great deal of difficulty for many children with perceptual-motor learning disabilities. Since, in a modern world, there are few opportunities to develop this skill, teachers must provide opportunities as a part of the regular school program. The development of laterality and directionality are also enhanced as children participate in balancing activities.

The following balancing activities are those children should practice before attempting ones that are more difficult. (Additional balancing activities are listed in the Fundamental Locomotor Movements and Stunt Activity sections.)

With feet together, children stand on tiptoes.

Children vary this by standing on tiptoes, each foot independently. They later repeat these activities with eyes closed.

Children stand on one foot, raise or swing the opposite foot forward, backward, or sideward.

They jump or hop (alternate feet) one step and maintain balance.

Teachers can use a chalk line, plastic floor marking tape, long jump ropes or existing painted lines for children to practice the following balance activities:

Children walk forward, backward, and sideward between two parallel lines six inches apart and at least eight feet long.

Children walk, forward and backward, with one foot on each line.

They walk on single lines, forward, backward, and sideward—right and left (step-together or cross-step).

They walk lines making half turns and full turns—both right and left.

Children walk lines that form various designs (use jump ropes).

ACTIVITIES INVOLVING A BALANCE BEAM

The balance beam is one of the most valuable pieces of apparatus for children with perceptual-motor learning disabilities. They are readily available through gymnastic equipment manufacturers or can easily be constructed (see Appendix).

Children should use rubber-soled gymnasium shoes or perform barefooted on the balance beam. They should practice specific stunts first on the floor. Teachers should hold the hand of a participant who is having difficulty, but remove this assistance as quickly as possible. Allow children who lose their balance to start again at the point where they stepped off.

Teach forward movements first. As children walk the beam, make sure each foot comes down accurately on the beam—both heel and toe touch on each step. At first, permit children to look at the beam as they walk. Later, as they develop more skill, move a pointer, yardstick, or wand five to six feet in front of each child as a target to sight on. Next, have children sight on the end of the beam as they cross. Finally, they should walk the beam without looking at it. In the appropriate location, place a target or picture on the wall for children to sight.

Instruct children to move slowly as they cross the balance beam; if they run it is possible to cross using a minimum of balancing action.

When moving backwards, permit children to look back over their shoulder. Most children will find this awkward, and after a short time they will keep their eyes straight ahead. Again a target or picture placed on the wall on which to sight will be helpful.

Sideward movements cause most difficulty. Teach children to keep the weight on the balls of the feet. They can cross in two ways—step together or the cross step.

When the activity involves a change of direction, ask children to turn both right and left.

The activities are listed in a suggested order of difficulty; however, teachers should not present the stunts in this order, but should select stunts that offer a variety of movements, positions and directions.

Walk forward or backward on the balance beam, arms held sideward. Vary by placing the arms and hands in many positions; e.g. hands on hips, arms extended in front or over head, arms folded, fingers laced behind the head.

Walk to the middle of the beam, turn and return to the starting position.

Walk to the middle of the beam, turn and walk the remaining distance backward.

Walk sideward right or left.

Walk to the middle of the beam, turn and walk the remaining distance sideward right or left.

Walk forward or backward with the right foot always preceding the left—left always preceding the right.

Place an object (bean bag or eraser) at the middle of the beam. Walk forward, pick up the object and continue to the end.

Walk forward or backward to the midpoint, kneel on one knee, rise and continue to the end. Repeat, kneeling on the other knee.

Walk forward or backward with an eraser or bean bag placed on top of the head.

Place an eraser or bean bag at the midpoint of the beam. Walk to the object; pick it up; place it on top of the head; walk the remaining distance with the object balanced on top of the head.

Another child holds a pointer, yardstick, or wand about ten to fifteen inches above the midpoint of the balance beam. Walk forward, backward or sideward and step over the object.

The pointer, yardstick, or wand is held at about chin height. Walk forward, backward or sideward passing under it. Gradually lower the height.

Walk the beam forward or backward, arms extended sideward, palms up with an eraser or bean bag on the palm of each hand. Repeat, placing the object on the back of each hand.

Walk forward to the middle of the beam, kneel on right or left knee, extend opposite leg forward until heel is on the beam and knee is straight. Stand and walk to the end of the beam.

Gallop across the beam; use the opposite lead foot.

Hop on the right or left foot across beam.

Walk to the middle of the beam, stand on one foot, swing the opposite foot forward and backward.

Walk to the midpoint of the beam; do a right or left side support; stand and walk to the end of the beam.

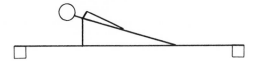

FIGURE 17

Place an eraser or bean bag at the middle of the beam. Walk to it; kneel; pick up the object and place it on the beam behind the performer; stand and continue to the end.

Perform a front scale—walk to the midpoint, stand on one foot, bend the trunk forward bringing trunk and free leg horizontal to the beam, arms held sideward. This activity also can be done from the knee.

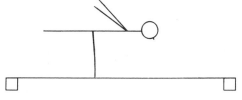

FIGURE 18

Place an eraser or bean bag at the midpoint of the beam; walk left sideward; pick up the object; place it on the right side of the beam; turn and walk right sideward to the end of the beam.

Another child holds a pointer, yardstick, or wand about fifteen inches above the beam. Place an eraser or bean bag on the head; walk forward, backward, or sideward (right or left), stepping over the object.

Place the hands on the beam. Have a partner hold the legs (wheelbarrow). Walk to the end of the beam, partner walking with his feet on the floor. Vary by having the partner also walk on the beam.

Do a "cat walk"—walk forward, backward, or sideward (left or right) on "all fours," hands and feet on the balance beam.

Walk to the midpoint of the beam, turn sideward and perform a Turk Stand—fold the arms and cross the legs, move to a deep squatting position, without using the hands, return to a standing position.

Perform an Inchworm Walk the length of the beam. (See page 62).

Perform a Crab Walk the length of the beam. (see page 60).

Play catch, throwing a bean bag to the child on the balance beam.

Rhythmic Activities

FIGURE 19

Children are exposed to a variety of rhythmic activities throughout their elementary school years—and beyond. Many children with perceptual-motor learning disabilities have difficulty in responding accurately to rhythms of various types.

After the children are having successful experiences with fundamental locomotor movements to rhythmic accompaniment (see pages 26–31), teachers can include more complex activities. Some of the traditional dance steps are valuable, not only because they aid in the development of rhythm, but also because they aid coordination and motor control.

When teaching these steps, let the children listen to the accompaniment in order to get an understanding of the quality and tempo of the rhythm. Have them clap the rhythm and verbalize the steps. Demonstrate the step. Allow the children to try the steps slowly, without the music. Increase the tempo and have them try the steps to music. Later they can use partners.

Some examples of traditional dance steps are as follows:

Step-hop:
    step on the left foot (count 1)
    hop on the left foot (count 2)
    step on the right foot (count 3)
    hop on the right foot (count 4)

With some children, start the skip at regular tempo, then slow the tempo until the skip becomes a step-hop. With other children it may be necessary to teach the step-hop slowly and mechanically, taking one foot at a time—step on the left foot, hop on it, etc.

Step-swing:
    step on the left foot (count 1)
    swing the right foot diagonally in front of the left (count 2)
    step right (count 3)
    swing the left foot diagonally in front of the right (count 4)

Vary by swinging the foot forward or sideward. When learning, have the children do the step-swing in place, later moving forward or backward using the step.

Bleking: Take two slow jump steps, followed by three in quick succession.
    jump with the right heel forward (count 1)
    hold (count 2)
    jump with the left heel forward (count 3)
    hold (count 4)
    jump right (count 1)
    left (count 2)
    right (count 3)
    hold (count 4)

Repeat starting with opposite foot.

Schottische:
    step right (count 1)
    step left (count 2)
    step right (count 3)
    hop right (count 4)

Repeat starting with the left foot. Start slowly, gradually increasing the speed until the first three steps are running steps.

Polka: (simplified version)
  step left (count 1)
  close right (count 2)
  step left (count 3)
  hold (count 4)

Repeat starting with the right foot.

Many singing games and folk dances, utilizing fundamental locomotor movements and traditional dance steps can be found in elementary physical education activity books (see Bibliography). Many of
these books indicate appropriate phonograph records to accompany
the specific dance activity.
  The following rhythmic activities appear because they are examples
of ones that may help in the development of body image or laterality.

Loobie Loo: (use Hokey Pokey for older children)
Formation: Single circle facing center, hands, joined.

Song:	Measures	Chorus
	1–2	Oh, here we go Loobie-Loo.
	3–4	Here we go Loobie-Light.
	5–6	Here we go Loobie-Loo,
	7–8	All on a Saturday night.
	1–2	1. I put my RIGHT HAND in.
	3–4	I take my right hand out.
	5–6	I give my hand a shake, shake,
	7–8	shake,
		And turn myself about.

2–9 Verses

2. I put my LEFT HAND in, etc.
3. I put BOTH HANDS in, etc.
4. I put my RIGHT FOOT in, etc.
5. I put my LEFT FOOT in, etc.
6. I put my ELBOWS in, etc.
7. I put my SHOULDERS in, etc.
8. I put my BIG HEAD in, etc.
9. I put my WHOLE SELF in, etc.

Action for Chorus: Circle left with walking steps.
Action for Verses 1–9:   Perform action of words. Start with chorus
and repeat chorus after each verse.

Did You Ever See a Lassie?
Formation: Single circle facing center, hands joined. One child in center.

Song:	Measures	Verse
	1–2	1. Did you ever see a lassie
	3–4	A lassie, a lassie?
	5–6	Did you ever see a lassie
	7–8	Go this way and that?
	1–2	2. Go this way and that way,
	3–4	Go this way and that way,
	5–6	Did you ever see a lassie
	7–8	Go this way and that?
		(Sing "laddie" when boy is in center.)

Action for part 1:   While singing, children circle left with walking steps (measures 1–8).
Action for part 2:   The child in the center rhythmically performs an action, imitation, or stunt. Others join in, imitating the leader. The center child chooses and changes places with the new leader. The children repeat the game with a new leader.

Through the tapping of hands and feet in a prescribed way, children are offered another way to develop rhythm. The teacher establishes the rhythmic pattern and the children listen to and attempt to repeat it, or the teacher establishes the pattern and, as soon as the children get the feel of the rhythm, they join with the teacher. Examples of patterns that can be used are as follows:

With the dominant hand or foot tap:

    right, right, right, etc.
    right (pause) right; etc.
    right, right (pause) right, right; etc.
    right, right, right (pause) right, right, right; etc.
    right (pause) right, right; etc.
    right, right (pause) right, right, right; etc.
    right, right, right (pause) right, right; etc.

Repeat with the non-dominant hand, foot, both hands, or both feet. When using the foot, tap the rhythm at some times using the toes and at other times using the heels. Later use the toes and heels alternately.

With children seated on the floor or on a chair have them clap their hands and pat their knees (use both hands), employing the following examples:

clap one; pat one; etc.
clap two; pat two; etc.
clap three; pat three; etc.
clap one; pat two; etc.
clap two; pat one; etc.

In time with the established rhythm, the children alternately tap hands or feet, for example:

right, left, right, left; etc.
left, left, right, right; etc.
right, left, left; etc.
left, right, right, right; etc.

Later add more complex activities combining hands and feet, for example:

Tap both hands and feet in time to prescribed rhythm.
Tap right hand and right foot.
Tap left hand and left foot.
Alternately tap both right hand and foot with left hand and foot.
Tap the right hand and left foot.
Tap the left hand and right foot.
Alternately tap right hand, left foot; left hand, right foot.

Stunt Activities

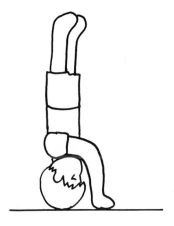

FIGURE 20

Most children greatly enjoy stunt activities as they delight in testing themselves when attempting new and exciting feats.

Stunt activities provide another avenue to help overcome the specific weaknesses of children with perceptual-motor learning disabilities. In addition to the familiar benefits of developing strength, balance, flexibility, agility, rhythm and coordination, with most of these activities it is necessary for children to move in unusual ways and in a variety of positions. There are many stunts that require children to isolate particular muscles, muscle groups, or body parts, thus assisting with a better understanding of body image. Other stunts are valuable in developing laterality, directionality, and spacial relationships.

GENERAL REMARKS ON FLOOR AND MAT STUNTS

Space does not allow for a complete discussion of stunt activities. Teachers should consult basic elementary physical education activity books for additional activities (see Bibliography). The stunts included are examples of those that will be valuable for children with perceptual-motor learning disabilities and with proper precautions, can be done on the floor as well as on mats. At the end of this section a list of activities appropriate for mats only will be given.

For safety children should take off eyeglasses if possible and remove unsafe articles from pockets or clothing.

Follow a progression of activities going from easy to more difficult, but know each child's strengths and limitations; do not allow children to try stunts that are too difficult.

Do all stunts away from walls, furniture, cupboards, etc.

Establish a definite routine for taking turns. Maintain an adequate space between performers. Specifically instruct children in how to fall, relaxing at the point of impact.

BOUNCE

From a standing position, feet together and hands on hips, have children bounce forward, backward or sideward (right and left).

Vary this by changing the position of the hands. For example, hands can be overhead, on shoulders, on top of the head, or fingers laced behind the neck. Hold only one hand overhead, alternate hands going overhead on each bounce.

Clap the hands in front or back on each bounce. Alternate clapping, front and back, on each bounce.

Bounce with feet apart and together, changing on each bounce. With older children involve the arms. For example, clap hands over head or touch the shoulders on each straddle.

Bounce in a zigzag fashion from side to side.

After each bounce turn right or left.

Alternate the feet on each bounce, apart, crossed, apart, crossed.

LOG ROLL

Have children lie on their stomach. Roll right or left by rotating the hips and shoulders in the direction of the movement. Vary the arm position; at sides, overhead, or folded across the chest.

SUPINE ROLLS

The children take a position on their backs, legs straight, feet together, arms at sides. They roll right or left to a hands-and-knees position; roll right or left to a hands-and-feet position.

CRAWL

From a position on the stomach have children move forward or backward by alternately using the right leg and left arm with the left leg and the right arm (cross-lateral).

Vary by having them move forward or backward alternately using the right arm and leg with the left arm and leg.

Have children move forward using only the arms and dragging the feet (Alligator Walk).

As the children move forward have them turn their heads from side to side watching the extended arm.

CREEP

From a hands-and-knees position repeat the activities listed for crawling.

When presenting crawling or creeping activities take care that children to not associate the crawling or creeping with the actions of babies. To assist with motivation, cut the ends out of cardboard boxes to serve as tunnels. Have children think of themselves as animals—a snake or worm or alligator. Let them pretend that they are hunters moving up stealthily on wild game.

ELEPHANT WALK

Have children bend forward from the waist, arms straight but not stiff, with the hands joined to represent a trunk. They swing the trunk from side to side with a heavy lumbering walk. To aid flexibility, have children keep the knees stiff and touch the fingertips to the floor on each step.

DOG WALK

The children should place their hands on the floor in front of the body keeping their knees and arms slightly flexed. Have children walk or run on all fours. Alternate using the right arm and left leg with the left arm and right leg. Vary this by alternately using the right arm and leg with the left arm and leg.

LAME DOG WALK

The children place their hands on the floor in front of the body, lifting one leg off of the floor and extending it backwards. They move forward by alternately walking on the hands and hopping with the foot. Have them repeat lifting the opposite foot from the floor.

KANGAROO JUMP

From a very erect squatting position with arms folded across the chest, children spring forcibly from the floor as high as possible and land easily on the balls of the feet. Continue the movement.

FROG JUMP

Have the children move to a squatting position, hands placed between or in front of the knees. They should spring vigorously bringing the entire body off of the floor, and then land in their original position. Encourage the children to increase the distance of each jump.

TURK STAND

The children start in a standing position with their arms and legs crossed. They then move to a sitting position without touching their knees or elbows to the floor. They lean forward and return to a standing position, again, without touching knees or elbows to the floor.

CRAB WALK

From a squatting position the children reach backward placing their hands on the floor, face up and with backs parallel to the floor. They walk forward, backward or sideward (right and left).

BEAR WALK

Have the children bend forward from the waist and place their hands on the floor. With heels flat on the floor and knees straight, they rock to the side on each step alternately moving the right arm and leg with the left arm and leg. Vary by using a cross-lateral movement.

RABBIT HOP

From a squatting position, the children place their hands between or in front of the knees. They spring forward by forcibly extending the knees, catching the weight on the hands, and then return the feet to the original position. Have children gradually increase the distance of each jump.

SEAL WALK

Have children take a regular push-up position and walk forward on their hands dragging the feet. Have them place the feet in various positions—crossed, heels together and toes out, or side-by-side.

TOE-TOUCH WALK

With the feet spread approximately fifteen inches apart, have children bend from the waist and touch the toes with the fingertips without bending the knees. They should then walk forward or backward keeping the fingers on the toes. Vary by crossing the arms.

TOP

The children stand, feet slightly astride and jump high attempting to make a complete turn without losing balance. They should rotate the head in the direction of the turn and use the arms to pull the body in the proper direction. Have the children start by jumping a quarter turn, a half turn, a three quarter turn before attempting a full turn, and let them practice turning both left and right.

INCHWORM WALK

From a push-up position, have the children keep their hands in place, knees straight, and walk the feet as close to the hands as possible. Keeping the feet in place, they should then walk with the hands back to the original push-up position.

BEAR BOUNCE

The children bend forward from the waist, placing their hands on the floor. The arms walk alternately forward, but the feet remain together and simultaneously take small bounces forward.

COFFEE GRINDER

The children take a push-up position; they side step with the feet and move right or left, the hands pivot in place. Repeat in a back-leaning position. Vary this by supporting the weight on either the right or left hand, keeping the body straight, and walking forward or backward in a circle around the supporting arm. The hand pivots as the body turns.

SNAIL

The children lie on their backs, legs straight and together, hands at sides, palms down. They move the legs overhead and touch the toes to the floor overhead, then return their legs to the original position.

COMBINE STUNTS

Combine single stunts into a sequence. Have children create combinations of stunts, for example, Bear Walk to Bear Bounce to Inchworm Walk; or Dog Walk to Elephant Walk to Bear Walk; or Bounce to Top to Turk Stand to Kangaroo Jump; or Crab Walk to Log Roll to Roll to Hands-and-Knees to Lame Dog Walk.

DO A DIFFERENT STUNT

Select a child to move in some way between two lines about fifteen feet apart. The next child must choose another way to move between the lines; the third a different way. Discuss the variety of ways the children invent to move.

STUNTS FOR MATS

The following stunts are more advanced and should be done on mats. Explanations can be found in most basic physical education activity books:

Forward and backward roll
Cartwheel
Dives
Headstand
Head and hand springs

ROPE STUNTS

There are many stunts that can be performed on the climbing ropes. They are uniquely valuable because most stunts are done within a new framework—off of the floor—with a new and different type of support. Only examples of basic ropes stunts will be described here, and teachers will probably wish to expand this list as children become more skilled.

SAFETY CONSIDERATIONS

Mats should be used under the ropes for all activities.

When children are swinging, insist that the ropes are stopped when the stunt has been completed.

Children should not slide on the ropes.

Know the children who may fear high places.

Children should maintain their hold on the rope until their feet are on the mat.

Establish a safety line, insist that no one crosses the line until it is their turn.

STRAIGHT ARM HANG

Have the children grasp the rope with both hands as high as possible above the head and hang. They can then do the following activities from the Straight Arm Hang:

Raise and lower both knees.
Raise and lower one knee independently (right and left).
Alternately raise and lower the knees.
Repeat these activities, but do not bend the knees.
Pull the chin to the hands.

As children gain more strength increase the number of repetitions.

Have children jump as high as possible and grasp the rope, elbow flexed or straight, and repeat the activities listed for Straight Arm Hang. If the ropes are paired, have the child grasp each rope as high as possible and repeat the activities listed for Straight Arm Hang.

THE ELEVATOR

Have the children grasp the rope at shoulder level with extended arms, feet on the mat about one foot apart. Keeping the body rigid and the feet in place they should lower the body moving hand under hand down the rope until the back rests on the mat. They can return to original position by pulling hand over hand.

THE MONKEY HANG

After grasping the rope at about eye level, the performer jumps and at the same time throws his head back, bringing the feet above the head. The feet cross around the rope over the hands. The body is in a tight tucked position.

For children having difficulty, start by having them lie on their backs and grasp the rope. They place the feet in the proper position around the rope and over the head. They then attempt to raise the body off the mat by pulling with the arms.

Next have the children try the Monkey Hang from a sitting position.

SKIN THE CAT

Paired ropes are needed for this stunt. The child grasps each rope at shoulder level, takes a slight jump pulling upward with the arms and throws the head back. He then flexes the knees bringing them close to the chest; his legs move backward between the ropes and downward to stand on the mat. Without releasing the grip, he returns to starting position by throwing the head forward between the knees, chin on the chest. He rolls forward, keeping knees close to the chest and returns the feet to the mat.

INVERTED HANG

The rope is grasped at about eye level. Keeping the rope at the side, the child gives a slight jump, throwing the head back and bringing the feet over the head to the rope. With one foot on each side of the rope, he pulls with the arms to straighten the body along the rope.

SWING

Have the children grasp the rope at shoulder level and walk back as far as possible. They jump and clasp the rope tightly with knees and ankles as it swings forward. When the children become more skillful, permit them to run forward with the rope and swing.

CLIMB

Before teaching the climb, children must first learn the proper foot grip. Grasping the rope with the hands as high as possible, they raise one knee and place the rope on the inside of the lifted knee and across the little toe side of the foot. They then pull with their arms to support the weight and bring the opposite foot in front of the rope and clamp the rope tightly between the outside edge of the feet, heels close together, toes parallel to floor.

Once the proper foot grip has been attained, have children grasp the rope as high as possible by climbing hand over hand. They should release the foot grip and slide the feet up the rope by flexing the knees. They can regrasp the rope using the foot grip. Have them continue alternately reaching with the arms and bringing the feet up the rope.

Children should descend by maintaining the proper foot grip and lowering the body hand under hand. Their knees and feet act as brakes.

Bean Bag and Ball Handling Activities

FIGURE 21

In our general society a great deal of prestige is given to those who can skillfully handle a ball. Competitive team games in school are a dominant part of the usual physical activity period. Not only is the ability to adequately handle a ball important for social recognition, but it is of great value in developing eye-hand and eye-foot coordination. Children with perceptual-motor learning disabilities need many experiences with balls of various sizes. The development of coordination is of great importance, but there are other benefits to be derived. These children learn to judge the speed and distance of a moving object. They receive valuable help with spacial relationships as they roll or throw a ball at a target. There are many opportunities for children to visually follow the movements of a moving object—a skill that many have great difficulty in accomplishing.

Teachers are cautioned to keep these activities as non-competitive as possible since many of these children have met failure and have been ridiculed for lack of ability. It may be necessary to group children until those having difficulty acquire the necessary skill.

BEAN-BAG ACTIVITIES

A bean bag is a very versatile piece of equipment. One of its primary values is that it is relatively easy to throw and is readily accepted by those who have difficulty catching because it does not hurt when it is missed. Some activities involving a bean bag are as follows:

Throw or toss a bean bag into a target marked on the floor. A bicycle tire makes an excellent target. Vary by throwing it into a container—a box or wastebasket. As children gain skill, the size of the target can be decreased or moved farther away.

Instruct children in a variety of ways to throw—underhand with both hands or one hand, overhand, one hand. See the sections on throwing listed under ball activities for an explanation of various throws.

PLAY LEADER AND CLASS

A small group of children (4–6) stand side by side facing a designated leader. The leader stands about ten feet in front of the class. Starting at one end of the line, he throws the bean bag in turn to each member of the class. Each player throws the bean bag back to the leader. As soon as each player in the group has had an opportunity to catch the bean bag and return it to the leader, the leader throws it to the first person in line who becomes the new leader. The old leader moves to the foot of the line. Continue the game until each child has been the leader. This is an activity to improve the skills of throwing and catching. There should be no penalty for a poor throw or failure to catch the bean bag. As skills improve increase the distance between leader and class. Engage in this activity for only short periods of time, not for the entire activity period.

Give a bean bag to all children in the class, and have them do the following:

1. Place the bean bag on the head and walk, run, skip, gallop, etc.
2. Place a bean bag on the back of each hand and walk, hop, jump, skip, etc.
3. Place the bean bag on the instep and walk. To add variety, have children swing the foot forward, backward, and sideward with the bean bag on the instep.

4. In a sitting, squatting or kneeling position, push the bean bag on the floor around the body.
5. Toss the bean bag up and catch it. Use two hands, one hand. Vary the height of the toss.
6. Throw the bean bag for distance.
7. Toss the bean bag overhead from hand to hand.
8. From a sitting or kneeling position, have children throw the bean bag in the air; quickly stand and catch it. From a standing position throw the bean bag up; move to a sitting or kneeling position and catch.
9. Stand, feet together, rest the bean bag equally on the insteps of each foot; jump and catch the bean bag.
10. Have children punt the bean bag (see explanation of punt under Ball Activities).

BALL ACTIVITIES

There is an abundance of games that involve balls of various weights and sizes. Teachers should refer to basic physical education activity books for games of this nature (see Bibliography).

Only fundamental ball handling skills will be described here. Some skills have been broken down into a step-by-step progression in order to help children who have difficulty with the particular activity.

LARGE BALL ACTIVITIES

THROWING A LARGE BALL
(SOCCER, VOLLEYBALL, BASKETBALL)

The following descriptions are for the right handed child.

There are some general principles to follow when teaching any type of throw with a large ball. The body is well balanced, feet in a stride position. The teacher should stress that when the ball is thrown with the right hand, the left foot should lead. The weight transfers from the right foot to the left foot for the follow-through. The throw is a smooth, coordinated, and continuous action of the arm and body. The eyes watch the target until the ball is released. The hand holding the ball should be slightly cupped, fingers apart. The opposite hand can be used to steady the ball before the throw.

ROLLING OR THROWING A BALL UNDERHAND
USING TWO HANDS

The ball can either be held to the right side or in front of the body. The hands are placed on opposite sides of the ball with palms facing, fingers apart and pointing down. As the ball swings forward quickly extend the wrist and elbows. At the same time, step forward on the left foot. To roll the ball, flex the knees to a greater extent than used in an underhand throw and release the ball on the ground.

THROWING A BALL OVERHAND USING TWO HANDS

The ball is held in two hands either directly overhead or over the shoulder. It is held with hands on opposite sides and palms facing, fingers apart and pointing up and back. The elbows are flexed and face the direction of the throw. The throw is a quick extension of wrists and elbows.

THROWING A BALL UNDERHAND USING ONE HAND

The ball is held to the side at about waist level. It is clamped firmly between the fingers and forearm of the throwing arm. The elbow and wrist are flexed. The opposite hand can be used to steady the ball. As the arm swings backward the weight shifts to the right foot and the body twists slightly to the right. As the ball swings forward it is kept close to the side, the weight now shifting forward onto the left foot. At the same time the elbow, wrist, and fingers are quickly extended.

THROWING A BALL OVERHAND USING ONE HAND

The ball is held over the shoulder, hand behind the ball, fingers apart and pointing up. The other hand can be used to steady the ball before the throw. The left side of the body is turned toward the target. As the arm is moved forward, the elbow extends and the wrist snaps forward; the weight transfers from the right foot to the left foot.

CATCHING A LARGE BALL

Many children have a fear of catching. Remove as much fear as possible by using a light 10″–12″ plastic ball or a soft 8½″–10″ playground ball. Release some air from a soccer ball, basketball or volleyball in order to remove anxiety.

When catching, place the feet in balanced stride position in order to move quickly in any direction. With the arms about waist high, flex the elbows slightly to form a basket with the chest and arms. Elbows must stay close enough together to prevent the ball from dropping between the arms. As the ball drops into the "basket," close the hands over the ball. At the same time relax and draw back with the ball. The eyes must remain open and watching the ball at all times.

When the ball does not come at chest level, teach children to spread the fingers, thumbs almost touching, and point them upward when catching a ball coming above the waist and to point them downward, little fingers almost touching, when catching a ball below the waist. Stress the importance of having the fingers relaxed and drawing back with the ball to bring it close to the body.

KICKING A STATIONARY BALL

In order for children who have difficulty with kicking to have a better chance for a successful experience use a durable, lightweight plastic ball or an inflatable soft-rubber playground ball. Later use the heavier, firm soccer ball.

The kicker should stand slightly to the left and behind the ball. The supporting foot should be to the side and from six to ten inches behind the ball. The leg swings backward with the knee flexed and then forward with a brisk extension of the knee, ankle rigid. The toe of the kicking foot should contact the ball on the upswing. After the impact the foot completes the follow-through, body balance being maintained. Stress keeping eyes open and watching the ball until it is kicked.

Use the following sequence when teaching this kick:

Have children stand in proper position and kick the ball.
Next have children take one step and kick.
Then children take several slow steps and kick.
Finally, have children gradually speed up and kick.

KICKING A ROLLING BALL

Kicking a rolling ball adds another dimension that is the cause of difficulty for some children. Now the kicker must align himself with the approaching ball and be able to judge its speed and level. He must retain his balance as he moves into position for the kick. As the kicker moves forward he must time the placement of the supporting foot (slightly to side and six to ten inches behind the ball) and maintain the established stride to get the full impact of the forward swing of the foot. Again, stress the importance of continually watching the ball until it is kicked.

Use the following sequence when teaching this kick:

Have children stand and wait for the ball and kick.
The children take one step and kick.
Take several slow steps and kick.
Have children start the approach as soon as the ball leaves the pitcher's hand.

There are many games that involve a pitcher. Vary the placement of the pitcher so the kicker must adjust to a ball coming from any direction.

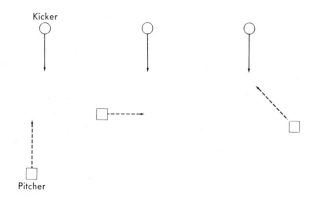

FIGURE 22

PUNTING A BALL

Use a light-weight ball when teaching the punt. The ball is held about waist high at arms length. The elbows are slightly bent and fingers are spread on opposite sides of the ball. In order to get more force into the kick teach children to take one or two steps before punting; i.e. step left, kick right or step right, step left, and kick right. The ball is dropped to contact the foot on the upswing. The foot meets the ball about knee high. The kick is made with the instep of the foot, toe is pointed. After contact, the follow-through is made by rising on the toe of the supporting foot. Trunk is erect, arms swing diagonally forward and upward for balance.

DROP KICKING THE BALL

The drop kick is similar to the punt, but is more difficult because of timing. The principle difference is that the ball hits the ground before the kick. The toe contacts the ball at the instant it bounces from the ground.

TRAPPING THE BALL

Trapping is a skill used in the game of soccer. It is stopping and gaining possession of a rolling or low bouncing ball without using the hands or arms. It involves aligning the body in the path of the approaching ball and using one of the following methods to stop and gain possession of the ball.

The player brings the sole of the foot down on top of the ball, but does not shift his weight to that foot. The toe is slightly higher than the heel so the ball is wedged between the ground and foot.

Another method of stopping the ball is the knee or shin trap. At the instant the ball touches the legs, the knees are flexed to wedge the ball between the shins and the ground. Either one or both knees can be used.

With both methods stress proper timing. Start by rolling the ball slowly to the trapper. Gradually increase the speed. Stress visually following the movement of the ball.

DRIBBLING THE BALL (SOCCER)

Dribbling is progressing the ball by a series of light taps or kicks with the sides of the feet. While running, the kicker attempts to keep the ball under control and a short distance in front as it is being advanced. Instruct children to start dribbling by walking with the ball, gradually increasing the speed until they are running. Teach children to rotate the legs outward and to tap the ball every few steps by the inside of alternate feet. The arms remain free to retain balance.

BALL ACTIVITIES INVOLVING VOLLEYBALL SKILLS

SERVING THE BALL

The right handed player stands with the left foot slightly advanced and pointing forward. Knees are relaxed, with slightly more weight on the right foot. The ball rests easily in the open left hand and is held across the body, about a foot in front of the right hip. As the right arm moves backward, the left hand remains in place. The shoulders twist a slight degree to the right; the right leg flexes and takes most of the weight. The right arm swings forward from the shoulder keeping the elbow and wrist straight. The weight is transferred from the right foot to the left foot as the ball is hit. The ball may be hit with the heel of an open hand or with the fist (either thumb side or the knuckles and heel). Children who are learning find more success with the fist serve using the surface formed by thumb and index finger. The right hand follows through to give the ball the appropriate height.

VOLLEYING

Volleying is a difficult skill to acquire. Due to the floating action, a large plastic beachball and a twelve inch plastic ball should be used before the regulation volleyball. The light plastic balls allow the children time to get their hands and body into position for the volley.

To volley a high ball the player stands with knees slightly flexed, feet apart. Elbows are flexed, wrists are extended as far as possible, palms face forward and upward, thumbs almost touch each other. As the ball is volleyed the elbows extend and wrist and fingers snap. The ball is played with finger tips. The player can add force by extending the knees and hips.

When volleying a low ball, the player stands with knees slightly flexed and feet apart. Elbows are almost fully extended, wrists are extended and palms face forward, little fingers are almost touching.

As the ball is volleyed the arms move upward from the shoulders, wrists and fingers snap upward. The player can add force by quickly straightening hips and knees.

Permit children to volley against a wall using different types of balls; volleyball, plastic, tennis, small rubber ball, etc. Start with the largest ball and progress to smallest one. Use the following sequence of activities:

Throw the ball against the wall and catch it on one bounce.
Throw the ball against the wall and catch it without a bounce.
Volley the ball against the wall.

Teachers should refer to basic physical education activity books for the dodgeball variety of games. Not only do these games aid in developing the skills of throwing and catching, but also dodging, changing direction, and visually following the action of the ball.

SMALL BALL ACTIVITIES

THROWING A SMALL BALL (SOFTBALL, TENNIS BALL)

Generally, the same basic principles are followed when throwing a small ball as those described for the large ball. Obviously the grip on the ball changes. A small ball is held with the fingers and thumb slightly spread. Avoid palming the ball.

CATCHING A SMALL BALL

Children should use a bean bag or fleece ball (see Appendix) when first learning to catch a small ball. Teach the children to extend the arms in the direction of the approaching ball, not a rigid extension. The arms, hands, and body should "give" or draw back to absorb the impact of the ball. The ball should be grasped by the fingers before it hits the heel of the hand. For a ball approaching waist level or above, fingers should point upward, thumbs touching. To catch a ball approaching below waist level, fingers point down, little fingers touching.

BATTING THE BALL

Batting is a skill that involves a great deal of motor control and coordination and may be especially difficult for children with perceptual-motor learning disabilities.

Instruct the children to stand with feet apart and parallel, toes pointing at the edge of home base closest to the batter. The distance from the base will vary with the length of the bat and the reach of the arm. The left side should face the playing field, the head toward the pitcher. Children should hold the bat securely with both hands; the right hand on top and touching the left hand, fingers and thumbs encircle the shaft. The bat is held away from the body; it does not rest on the shoulder. The left elbow is at about shoulder level; the tip of the bat points up and back. As the pitcher prepares to throw, the batter's weight transfers to the right foot. From this position the bat swings forward, parallel to the ground. The arms are straight. As the bat travels forward, the weight shifts to the left foot. The follow-through carries the bat forward and past the left shoulder, horizontal to the ground.

Use the following progression to teach batting:

Have batter hit a stationary ball resting on a batting tee (see Appendix). First use a plastic bat and ball; later use a regular bat and ball.

Use a player to turn a tetherball in a circular manner so that the ball travels between knee and shoulder height. The batter attempts to hit the moving ball. As the skill improves, tie a rope to a plastic ball (softball size), rotate the ball in the same way. The batter attempts to hit the smaller target.

Now pitch an old volleyball in the same manner used in softball.

Finally pitch a regular softball at a very slow speed, gradually increasing the speed.

BALL ACTIVITIES INVOLVING BOUNCING

Use balls of various sizes for the following activities. Start with a large ball and progress to smaller ones.

When teaching ball bouncing, have children push the ball down using the finger tips. The ball should not be slapped or hit downward. Have children bounce the ball with two hands and catch it. Vary by bouncing the ball with two hands—no catch, bounce with the right hand, the left hand and, alternate hands.

Bounce the ball using various patterns, for example, right, right, left, left, etc.; or left, left, right, etc.; or right, right, right, left, left, etc.

Bounce the ball slow, fast, high, low, heavy, or soft.

Bounce the ball while moving forward, backward, and sideward.

Bounce the ball while skipping, hopping, running, etc.

Bounce the ball around the body or under the leg.

Toss the ball up and catch it on two bounces, one bounce, or no bounces.

Toss the ball up, run under it, turn to the right or left and catch it, two bounces, or one bounce. Vary by turning right or left one and a half turns.

In a sitting, squatting, or kneeling position, throw up the ball, stand and catch it; while standing throw up the ball, move to the original position and catch the ball.

See Jack Activities in the section on Auxiliary Activities for additional small ball activities.

Obstacle Course

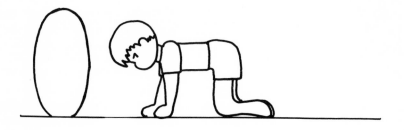

FIGURE 23

An obstacle course can be arranged in most locations; gymnasium, classroom, cafeteria, hall or outside play area. Obstacle courses enable a large number of children to participate in a wide variety of activities in a short span of time. Activity sites can be established utilizing any of the activities previously listed or those described in the Auxiliary Activities section. Teachers can use as little or as much equipment as necessary to meet the needs of the class and still safely adjust to the size of the facility.

Teachers should give a brief description of the activities at each site, and divide the class into small groups (no more than four or five at an activity site). After a specified amount of time, on signal, the children rotate to the next site. The teacher should move freely to each activity area and give as much individual help as possible.

Another important aspect of the obstacle course arrangement is that there is a freedom on the part of the children to attempt new activities because everyone is actively participating, leaving very little time for observing or making comments about the performance of others.

The activities to be included are unlimited. The following are examples of obstacle courses that can be located in the classroom, the gymnasium, or on the outside play area.

CLASSROOM

The modern classroom has a great deal of flexibility. In most cases desks, tables and chairs can be easily moved to accommodate the obstacle course. Furniture can be moved to the center of the room leaving the outside perimeter, available or it can be moved to the outer edges leaving a large area in the center of the room.

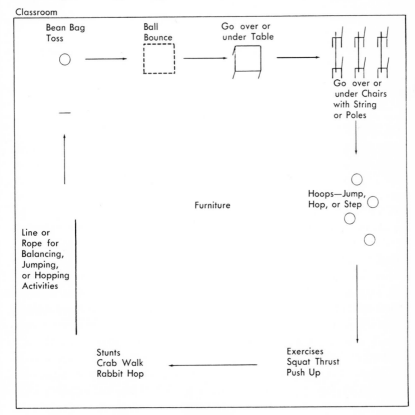

FIGURE 24

Gymnasium • Playroom • All Purpose Room

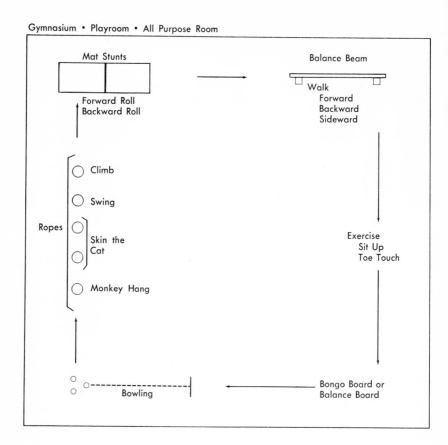

FIGURE 25

Outdoor Play Area

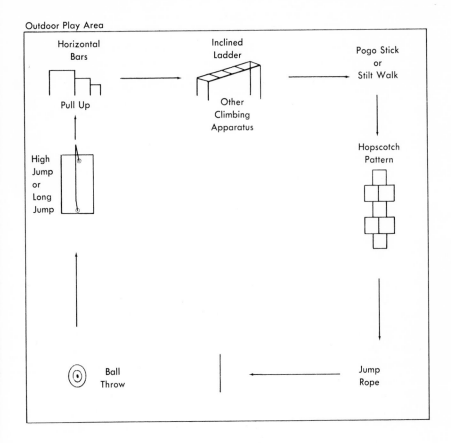

FIGURE 26

Movement Exploration

FIGURE 27

Movement exploration can utilize the many activities previously described in the various sections; the teacher's *approach* to the activity is the significant factor. Instead of the traditional approach (a verbal explanation, a demonstration by teacher or child, an attempt by all, an evaluation, and another attempt) the teacher gives a problem to be solved by movement. Each child, in his *own* way, finds the solution to the problem. Through this problem-solving approach children discover that they can make countless movements in many positions and postures, either while stationary or when moving through space.

The teacher does not demonstrate the movement or give any clue to solving the stated problem. As children progress the problems become more complex, or if children have difficulty, the teacher restates the problem to get at the planned objective. The teacher expects and encourages individual responses to questions.

Since the children solve the problems in their own ways, each will have a successful experience. Also, children can enhance the understanding of their body movement potential, its capabilities and limitations, and discover that these may differ from their classmates.

Through well-planned movement exploration experiences, children can increase their understanding of space including direction—up, down, forward, backward; level—high, low; and range—big movement, small movement.

Teachers can assist children in developing a better understanding of quality of movement whether it is fast or slow, light or heavy, sustained or explosive. Children can be given problems concerning balance; locomotor movements, e.g., walking, hopping, skipping, galloping, etc.; non-locomotor movements, e.g., twisting, stretching, bending, shaking, striking, etc.

Equipment can be used to reinforce some movement concepts or may add a completely new dimension. A variety of equipment is an integral and vital part of the movement exploration experience.

The examples serve only as a starting point and should in no way limit the creativity of the teacher.

PROBLEMS INVOLVING BODY MOVEMENT

How tall (short, big, small, fat, thin, straight, crooked) can you be?

Can you make yourself flat (round, bumpy)?

Who can make himself little and round (tall and thin)?

While sitting (standing, lying, kneeling, etc.) how many ways can you move your head (shoulders, arms, elbows, hands, hips, legs, knees, toes, etc.)?

PROBLEMS INVOLVING NON-LOCOMOTOR MOVEMENTS

PUSH AND PULL

How would you push something away?

How would you pull something to you?

Show us another way to push (pull).

Can you push (pull) fast? Slow?

Push (pull) something that is very heavy.

FALL AND RISE

While standing (sitting, kneeling, lying) raise one (two, three) part(s) of your body.

While standing (sitting, kneeling, lying) let one (two, three) part(s) fall.

Who can raise his arms level with his shoulders? Let me see them fall to your side. While lying on your back, can you lift one (two) legs? How fast can it fall?

SWING AND SWAY

Can you swing your arms? Swing them another way.

Can you make your body, from the waist up, sway to the side (back and forth)?

Swing one (two, three) part(s) of your body.

While standing (sitting, kneeling, lying) what parts of your body can you swing (sway)?

Who can swing their leg fast (slow)?

BEND AND STRETCH

Show how you can bend (stretch) every part of your body.

Who can bend (stretch) one (two, three) part(s) of his body?

At a low (medium, high) level stretch (bend) your arms. Who can bend (stretch) very quickly (slowly)?

Show how you can make a big (small) bending (stretching) movement.

TWIST AND TURN

Who can twist their wrist (head, shoulder, leg, feet, etc.)?

Show how you can twist one (two, three) part(s). Untwist one (two, three) part(s).

Turn your body when you are at a high (medium, low) level.

Can you twist one part of your body quickly while another is twisting slowly?

SHAKE

Can you shake your head (shoulders, hands, legs) while standing (sitting, kneeling, lying)?

Show how you can shake one (two, three) part(s).

Show a big (small) shaking movement.

Can you show a fast (slow) shaking movement? Use another part of your body.

BOUNCE

Show how you can bounce your head (feet, shoulders, knees).
While standing (sitting, kneeling, lying) what can you bounce?
Bounce a big (small) part of your body.
Bounce one (two, three) part(s).
Can you make a big (small) bounce?
At a low (medium, high) level make a slow (fast) bouncing movement.

PROBLEMS INVOLVING LOCOMOTOR MOVEMENTS

WALK

Can you walk in different directions? (Forward, backward, sideward?)
Can you walk on different parts of your feet? (Your tiptoe, heel?)
Show how you can take high (low, short, long, heavy, light) steps as you walk.
Walk in a crouched position and gradually rise to an erect walking position.
In what different positions can you place your arms as you walk?
Can you walk slowly (fast)?

RUN

Show how you can take high (low) steps while you are running.
How fast (slow) can you run?
From a low (medium) level come to an erect running position and return to a low (medium) level.
Run with heavy (light) steps.

JUMP

Show how high (low, long, short) you can jump.
Show how your arms can help you jump.
In what directions can you jump? (Forward, backward, sideward [right and left]?)
How fast (slow) can you jump?

Can you take two fast jumps and three slow jumps?
How far can you jump starting with your feet together?
Can you jump and land on one foot and hold your balance?

HOP

How high (low, long, short, heavy, light) can you hop?
In what directions can you hop? (Forward, backward, sideward [right and left]?)
Can you hop at a low (medium) level?
Show what you can do with the other foot as you hop.
Can you hop fast on one foot, change, and hop slowly on the other?
Can you hop three times on one foot and four times on the other?

SKIP

Show a fast (slow, heavy, light) skipping step.
Can you start skipping very slowly gradually going faster and faster?
What can you do with your arms as you skip?
Show me a high (low) skipping step.
Skip in different directions.

GALLOP

In how many directions can you gallop?
How fast (slow, long, short) can you gallop?
Gallop first with one foot leading, then the other.
Can you gallop with heavy steps with one foot leading and light steps with the other foot leading?
What can you do with your arms as you gallop?

SLIDE

Can you slide at a high (medium, low) level?
Can you start at a low level and gradually move to a high level as you slide?

Who can take five slides in one direction and three in another direction?

Show how fast (slow, long, short) you can slide.

MOVEMENT PROBLEMS INVOLVING
THE CHILDREN'S IMAGINATION

Can you be a big (small) bird flying?
What kind of animal can you be?
Show us how you can row a boat.
Be a clock ticking.
Can you spin like a top?
Be a fast (slow) train.
Can you be rain (snow) falling?
How would you be a lawn mower?
Be a sack of sugar with a small hole in the end.
Show how you would be a tractor pulling (pushing) a heavy load.
Be a feather floating in the wind.

MOVEMENT PROBLEMS INVOLVING
ACCESSORIES AND EQUIPMENT

Can you walk to the midpoint of the balance beam, kneel on one knee, stand, and walk backwards to the starting point?

Who can walk sideward on the balance beam with a bean bag on their head? What else can you do with the bean bag?

While balancing on one foot in the middle of the balance beam, what can you do with the other foot?

Who can jump the rope ten times? Can you do it while turning the rope backwards?

With a rope stretched straight on the floor, can you jump (hop) in a zigzag fashion the entire length of the rope landing first on one side of the rope and then on the other?

How many ways can you move to the line as you jump the rope?

Who can throw the bean bag high and still catch it?

How many ways can you kick the bean bag?

Show how you can throw the bean bag overhead and catch it with the other hand.

Who can bounce the ball using one hand, then the other?

How can you move the ball to the line without touching it with your hands?

Can you throw the ball up and catch it on the second bounce (first bounce, before it bounces)?

Other problems can be given while using stilts, pogo sticks, hula hoops, chairs, tables, etc.

Auxiliary Activities

FIGURE 28

Children with perceptual-motor learning disabilities need a wide variety of movement experiences. Included in the regular physical activity period should be supplemental activities that not only add to or reinforce previous experiences, but also aid in motivating the children.

Children with perceptual-motor problems should be encouraged to participate in many of the auxiliary activities outside of the regular physical activity period. Usually playground equipment, tetherball, jacks and hopscotch are available before school, at noon and after school. Parents should be informed of the value of some auxiliary activities in order for them to assist their children in overcoming specific weaknesses.

PLAYGROUND EQUIPMENT

Most schools have a variety of playground equipment. Children need to make adjustments to distances, heights, widths, and inclines as they hang, climb, go under, go over, in front of, and behind, on a variety of equipment. They need to make judgments about speed and rhythm and develop the necessary timing to successfully participate on equipment that has moving parts. Children not only can aid their physical fitness, but they develop motor control and coordination as they perform stunts in many different positions on playground apparatus.

Playground equipment activities should not be a "free play time" for children. Frequently, teachers should assign specific tasks to each piece of apparatus.

TETHERBALL

Tetherball has not only become a piece of equipment found on many school playgrounds, but it is not unusual to find this equipment at local residences. It is an excellent activity for children with perceptual-motor learning disabilities because it can be of great value in aiding the development of eye-hand coordination. The eyes must follow the movements of the ball; the hands must strike the ball with precise timing. It is important for players to make quick judgments as to the speed and elevation of the ball as it rotates around the pole.

Teachers should permit some children to practice the necessary skills alone before they participate in a regular game. Many children who could benefit from the activity avoid it because of consistent defeat. These children should have opportunities to practice striking the ball with two hands, the right hand or the left hand as it rotates in both directions around the pole.

The rules of tetherball can be found in many basic physical activity books (see Bibliography).

HOPSCOTCH

Hopscotch is one of the traditional activities that interest children both at school and in the neighborhood. A variety of patterns, differing in complexity, are available. Many schools with blacktopped areas have a variety of permanent painted hopscotches.

Like many other activities, with some children, teachers must do much more than present the rules of the game. A well-planned sequence of steps is necessary before some children will wish to play hopscotch voluntarily. Hopscotch is a valuable activity since it involves making spacial judgments, balancing, and controlling movements.

Teachers can have children review many of the hopping and jumping activities described under Fundamental Locomotor Movements before starting any phase of hopscotch. After these preliminaries, start with a single square, the sides being approximately fifteen inches, (larger for those having difficulty). Have children jump in and out, then hop in and out using both the right foot and the left foot. Use the following patterns to develop skills before playing the game. Involve both hopping and jumping.

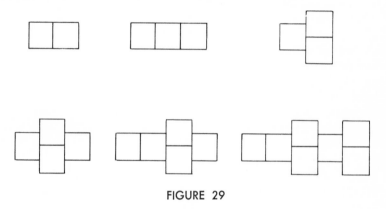

FIGURE 29

The most basic game of hopscotch uses the following pattern:

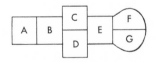

FIGURE 30

Each section is about fourteen inches in depth.

One to four children can play the game. Each player has an object (puck, rock, bottle cap, bean bag) to toss into the spaces. A hop is necessary for space A, B, and E. A jump is required for C-D and F-G if no puck is resting within them.

The first player stands on the starting line (the front line of space A) and tosses his puck into space A. He then hops over A landing in space B, jumps into C-D, hops into E and jumps into F-G. He jumps one-half turn to face the starting line. He returns with a hop into E, a jump into C-D, a hop into B. He then picks up his puck, hops into A and out.

The player then tosses his puck into B, hops into A, jumps over B landing in C-D, hops into E and continues as before. On the return trip he picks up his puck before hopping into B.

A player misses when he commits one of the following violations:

1.   stepping on a line with any part of the foot
2.   permitting the elevated foot to touch the ground except in spaces C-D and F-G
3.   throwing the puck into the incorrect space. Pucks landing on the line are considered good.
4.   losing the balance and contacting the ground with the hands as the puck is being retrieved
5.   failing to hop or jump into the correct spaces or hopping or jumping into a space containing a puck

A player who misses loses his turn and places his puck into the space he missed. On his next turn the player must start at the beginning of the series he missed. The first player who tosses the puck into G and completes the pattern without a miss is the winner.

SUPPLEMENTAL BALANCING EQUIPMENT

To add variety to the balancing activities previously described, four items of equipment are appropriate. When children have reached the proper skill level they should have opportunities to work on stilts, pogo sticks, balance board or Bongo Board.

STILTS (SEE APPENDIX)

When the children are learning to walk on stilts, the stilts' foot platforms should be no more than six to ten inches from the ground. Children should walk forward, backward and sideward.

BALANCE BOARDS AND BONGO BOARDS (SEE APPENDIX)

Children attempt to balance without allowing the ends or edges of the boards to touch the ground. Place a mat or piece of rug under the Bongo Board to slow the action.

POGO STICK

Have the children start with small bounces in place gradually bouncing higher and adding movement forward, backward and sideward.

FLOOR DOLLIES OR SCOOTERS (SEE APPENDIX)

Due to the interest and enjoyment children derive from activities on the floor dollies, they serve as another avenue to attack weakness in laterality, directionality, body image, motor control and spacial relationships.

Have children use the following positions and actions:

1. Sit on the dolly facing the front. Use the heels bilaterally or alternately to pull forward.
2. Sit on the dolly. Use the heels to push backwards—bilateral or alternate foot action.
3. Sit on the dolly with legs crossed. Use the arms, bilaterally or alternately to pull forward.
4. Kneel on the dolly and use the hands to pull forward. Again, the hand action can be bilateral or alternate.
5. Kneel with one knee on the dolly, hands holding the sides of the dolly. Use the free foot to move. Repeat using the opposite foot.
6. Lie in a prone position on the dolly, hands holding the edges of the dolly, and use the feet to move forward—bilateral or alternating action of feet.
7. Lie in a prone position on the dolly. Use the arms bilaterally or alternately to move forward.

JACKS

Jacks is another of the games that has been enjoyed by children for many years. It is especially valuable because it can aid children with perceptual-motor learning disabilities in eye-hand coordination. Jacks also can assist with an understanding of rhythm, timing and making accurate spacial judgments.

Teacher should review with children the bouncing activities listed in the section on Bean Bag and Ball Handling Activities preliminary to the following sequence:

1. Sit, legs wide apart, or kneel. Progress from a tennis ball to a smaller ball.
2. Toss the ball up and catch it on one bounce.
3. Toss the ball up, clap the hands one (two, three, four) time(s) and catch it on one bounce.
4. Toss the ball up, slap the floor with both hands one (two, three, four) time(s) and catch it on one bounce.
5. Toss the ball up, clap the hands, slap the floor with both hands and catch it on one bounce. Gradually increase the number of claps and slaps.
6. Toss the ball up with the right hand and catch it with the right hand on one bounce. Repeat this with the left.
7. Toss the ball up with the right hand, slap the floor with the right hand, and catch the ball with the right hand. Repeat this with the left hand. Increase the number of slaps on the floor.

Use many combinations. For example, toss the ball up with the right hand and catch it with the left hand on one bounce; or toss the ball up with the left hand, slap the floor with the left hand, and catch the ball with the right hand on one bounce; or toss the ball up with the right hand, slap the floor with the left hand, and catch the ball with the left hand.

After children have had an opportunity to do many of the tasks listed above, most will enjoy the regular game of Jacks. At first use only a small number of jacks, gradually increasing the number.

The first player scatters the jacks, throws the ball up, picks up one jack and catches the ball in the hand holding the jack. The ball must be caught on the first bounce.

He puts the jack into the other hand and continues picking up all the jacks one at a time. If he is successful in picking up all the jacks, he scatters the jacks again. This time he picks up two at a time. The next time three and so on.

A player misses and loses his turn when he commits one of the following violations:

1. dropping one or more jacks
2. missing the ball
3. touching a jack when not attempting to pick it up
4. picking up the incorrect number of jacks
5. catching the ball with the wrong hand
6. permitting the ball to bounce more than once

When the player who misses again has his turn, he must start with the series he previously missed. The first player to complete all games, finally picking up all of the jacks and catching the ball correctly is the winner.

CHALKBOARD ACTIVITIES

Chalkboard activities not only are helpful in assisting children with the development of laterality, directionality and eye-hand coordination, but can serve as a valuable method of identifying children who have perceptual-motor learning disabilities.

Start the children with circles. Center the children in front of the chalkboard, far enough back so their wrists cannot touch. Have the children draw a circle about 20 inches in diameter going both clockwise and counterclockwise and using first the dominant hand and then the non-dominant hand.

Instruct the children to take a piece of chalk in each hand. Have them draw a circle with each hand about 20 inches in diameter moving the right hand counterclockwise and the left hand clockwise and reverse. They then move both hands counterclockwise and reverse.

Have children draw lines. Place two dots about 20 inches apart so children will draw a horizontal line between dots. They move their hands right to left then left to right, first using the dominant hand, then the non-dominant. Repeat placing the dots so children will have to make vertical lines between the dots. They move their hands from top to bottom and from bottom to top. Repeat placing the dots so children will have to move the hand in a diagonal direction.

Use a lettered circle.

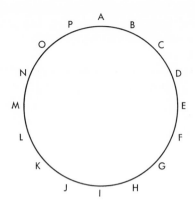

FIGURE 31

There are a great number of combinations that can be used:

From edge to center. For example, place the left hand on K, right hand on C, and move hands to the center dot simultaneously.

From center to edge. For example, place both hands at the center and move hands simultaneously, the left hand to H the right hand to A.

From edge and center. For example, place right hand on D, left hand on center; the right hand moves to center, the left hand moves to M. Repeat actions with left hand on center.

Alternate action from edge and center. For example, place the left

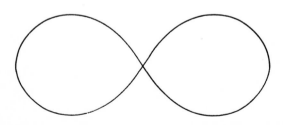

FIGURE 32

hand on J, the right hand on center; the left hand moves to center, the right hand stays in place until the left hand action is complete. Then the right hand independently moves to B.

Have children do the Lazy Eight. Make a horizontal eight on the board approximately 24 inches long and 12 inches wide. Instruct children to move in both directions using the dominant hand then the non-dominant hand. See Figure 32.

Glossary

Bilateral: Movements of both sides of the body that are simultaneous and parallel.

Body Image: An understanding of the movement and performance capabilities of one's own body.

Cross-lateral: Simultaneous movement of different limbs on opposite sides of the body or the simultaneous movement of the same limbs. For example, moving both legs but in opposite directions.

Directionality: An understanding of left and right, down and up, over and under, front and behind, etc., developing first from an internal awareness and then into external space. (Laterality develops before directionality.)

Dominance: The preferred side of the body in reference to the hand, foot, eye.

Fine motor skills: Activities that demand precise and delicate muscle performance.

Gross Motor Skills: Activities that put into play large muscle groups.

Laterality: An internal awareness of the two sides of the body and the facility to use each side separately or both sides at the same time.

Midline: An imaginary line separating the right and left sides of the body—the body's center of gravity.

Perceptual-Motor: Muscular activity as a result of sensory stimulation.

Spacial orientation: The relationship between the individual and an object or between objects.

Unilateral: Movements using one side of the body.

Bibliography

LEARNING DISABILITIES

Barsch, R. H. "A Movigenic Curriculum." *Bulletin No. 25*, University of Wisconsin, Madison, Wisconsin: State Department of Public Instruction, 1965.

Chaney, C. M. and Kephart, N. C. *Motoric Aids to Perceptual Training.* Columbus, Ohio: Charles E. Merrill Books, Inc., 1968.

Clements, S. D. *Minimal Brain Dysfunction in Children.* Washington, D.C.: United States Department of Health, Education and Welfare, 1966.

Cruikshank, W. and Others. *A Teaching Method for Brain Injured and Hyperactive Children.* Syracuse, N.Y.: Syracuse University Press, 1961.

Frostig, M. *Movement Education: Theory and Practice.* Chicago, Ill.: Follett Publishing Company, 1970.

Getman, G. N. *How to Develop Your Child's Intelligence.* Minnesota: G. N. Getman, Luverne, 1962.

Getman, G. N. and Kane, E. R. *The Physiology of Readiness.* Minneapolis, Minnesota: P.A.S.S., Inc., 1964.

Godfrey, B. B. and Kephart, N. C. *Movement Patterns and Motor Education.* New York: Appleton-Century-Crofts, 1969.

Gordon, Sol and Golub, R. S. *Recreation and Socialization for the Brain Injured Child.* New Jersey: New Jersey Association for Brain Injured Children, 1966.

Johnson, D. J. and Myklebust, H. R. *Learning Disabilities*. New York: Grune and Stratton, 1967.

Kephart, N. C. *The Slow Learner in the Classroom*. Columbus, Ohio: Charles E. Merrill Books, Inc., 1960.

Kephart, N. C. *Learning Disability: An Educational Adventure*. West Lafayette, Ind.: Kappa Delta Pi Press, 1968.

Roach, E. G. and Kephart, N.C. *The Purdue Perceptual Motor Survey*. Columbus, Ohio: Charles E. Merrill Books, Inc., 1966.

PHYSICAL EDUCATION

Andrews, G. and Others. *Physical Education for Today's Boys and Girls*. Boston: Allyn and Bacon, 1960.

Bilbrough, A. and Jones, P. *Physical Education in the Primary School*. London: University of London Press, Ltd., 1968.

Cochran, N. A. and Others. *A Teacher's Guide to Elementary School Physical Education*. Dubuque, Iowa: William Brown Book Co., 1967.

Dauer, V. P. *Dynamic Physical Education for Elementary School Children*. Minneapolis, Minnesota: Burgess Publishing Co., 1968.

Dauer, V. P. *Fitness for Elementary School Children*. Minneapolis, Minnesota: Burgess Publishing Co., 1962.

Diem, L. *Who Can*. Frankfort A.M., Germany: Wilhelm Limpert Publisher, 1955. Copyright U.S.A., George Williams College, 1957.

Donnelly, R. and Others. *Active Games and Contests*. New York: Ronald Press Co., 1958.

Fait, H. F. *Physical Education for the Elementary School Child*. Philadelphia: W. B. Saunders Co., 1964.

Hackett, L. C. and Jenson, R. G. *A Guide to Movement Exploration*. Palo Alto, California: Peck Publications, 1966.

Halsey, E. and Porter, L. *Physical Education for Children: A Developmental Program*. New York: Dryden Press, 1958.

Horne, V. L. *Stunts and Tumbling for Girls*. New York: A. S. Barnes and Co., 1943.

Jones, E., Morgan, E. and Stevens, G. *Methods and Materials in Elementary Physical Education*. Yonkers, New York: The World Book Co., 1957.

Kirchner, G. *Physical Education for Elementary School Children.* Dubuque, Iowa: William Brown Publishers, 1970.

Kulbitsky, O. and Kaltman, F. R. *Teachers Dance Handbook, Number One, Kindergarten to Sixth Year.* New Jersey: Bluebird, 1959.

LaSalle, D. *Rhythms and Dance for Elementary Schools.* New York: A. S. Barnes, 1951.

Miller, A. and Whitcomb, V. *Physical Education in the Elementary School Curriculum.* Englewood Cliffs, New Jersey: Prentice-Hall, Inc., 1957.

Moston, M. *Developmental Movement.* Columbus: Charles E. Merrill Book Co., 1965.

Moston, M. *Teaching Physical Education.* Columbus: Charles E. Merrill Book Co., 1966.

Murray, R. L. *Dance in Elementary Education: A Program for Boys and Girls.* New York: Harper-Row, 1963.

Neilson, N. P. and Others. *Physical Education for Elementary Schools.* New York: Ronald Press Co., 1966.

O'Quinn, G. *Gymnastics for Elementary School Children.* Dubuque, Iowa: William C. Brown Publishers, 1967.

Salt, E. B. and Others. *Teaching Physical Education in the Elementary School.* New York: Ronald Press, 1960.

Shurr, E. L. *Movement Experiences for Children: Curriculum and Methods for Elementary School Physical Education.* New York: Appleton-Century-Crofts, 1967.

Vannier, M. and Foster, M. *Teaching Physical Education in Elementary Schools.* Philadelphia: W. B. Saunders Co., 1963.

Appendix

EQUIPMENT

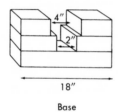

18″

Base

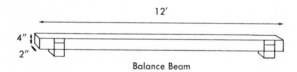

12′

4″
2″

Balance Beam

FIGURE 33

12″ Diameter
Fleece Ball

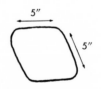

5″

5″

Bean Bag

FIGURE 34

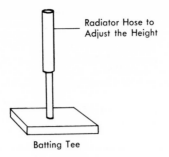

FIGURE 35

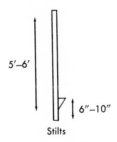

FIGURE 36

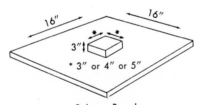

FIGURE 37

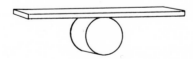

FIGURE 38

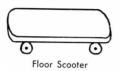

Floor Scooter

FIGURE 39

Index